This book is dedicated to our LEGO® loving children
who inspired all these wonderful learning ideas.

A Note About Safety:

The activities in this book are intended to be done under adult supervision. Appropriate and reasonable caution is required at all times. The authors of this book disclaim all liability for any damage, mishap or injury that may occur from engaging in activities in this book.

Copyright:

Disclaimer:

These activities are not instructions and are open to creative interpretation.

The authors of this book are not affiliated with any of the products used or displayed.

LEGO®is a trademark of the LEGO Group of companies which does not sponsor, authorize or endorse this book.

Meet the Authors

Danielle Buckley

Danielle is a former teacher and stay-at-home mom of two active preschoolers. She enjoys sharing playful learning activities and neat ideas that keep her kids engaged and having fun!

http://www.mominspiredlife.com

Nicolette Roux

Nicolette is a stay at home mom to 4 little ones. She loves to share her simple and easy crafts & activities, printables and learning ideas on her blog!

http://www.powerfulmothering.com

Dayna Abraham

Dayna is a National Board Certified early childhood teacher turned homeschooling mom of three who's mission is to remain down to earth while providing ideas for intentional learning experiences ranging from science to sensory play.

http://www.lemonlimeadventures.com

Samantha Soper-Caetano

Samantha is a stay-at-home mom to an active preschooler. She loves thinking of creative ways to engage her son in hands-on learning, including fine motor activities, sensory play, nature exploration, science experiments, and book-inspired ideas!

http://www.stirthewonder.com

Laura Marschel

Laura is mom to two sweet redheads who fuel all the fun on her blog. She shares cool kids crafts, fun activities, free printables and parenting tips too! It's basically all about having fun!

http://www.lalymom.com

Sarah McClelland

Sarah is a stay-at-home mom of one busy boy. She enjoys incorporating important fine motor skills practice into a variety of hands-on learning activities that her son enjoys. Sarah's blog focuses on science, sensory, and STEM activities for learning and play.

http://www.littlebinsforlittlehands.com

Contents

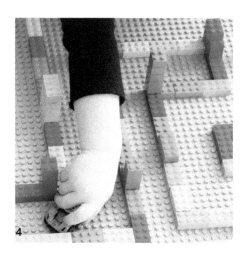

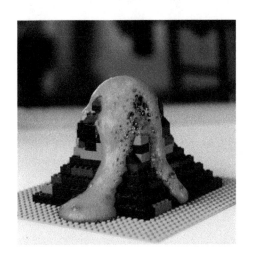

Duplo Ring Toss

Materials / Supplies

- Pipe cleaners
- Duplo plate
- Duplo 2x2 bricks (50+)

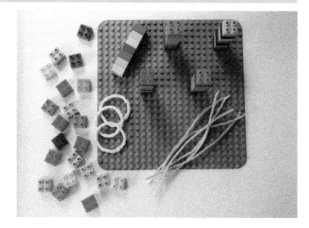

Instructions

Building Duplo towers and twisting pipe cleaners into rings is really good for fine motor skills.

Preschoolers can count how many rings they get on the Duplo towers. By placing numbers on the Duplo towers, older children can add up points and keep score.

1. To make the rings to toss, twist three pipe cleaners together and form a circle.
2. Create eight or more towers by stacking six or seven 2x2 Duplo bricks into a tower.
3. Attach the Duplo towers, evenly spaced onto the Dupo plate to make a ring toss stand.
4. Set the ring toss stand on the floor or low table.
5. Have the children take turns tossing the rings onto the Duplo towers.

Skills:
Fine Motor, Math

Writing Your Name with Bricks

Materials / Supplies

- 1x8 bricks
- 1x6 bricks
- 2x4 bricks
- 2x2 bricks

Instructions

While doing this activity, children will practice letter recognition and letter formation. This is essential to learning to read and write. They will also learn to spell their own name.

1. Use the 1x8 and 1x6 bricks to build each of the letters of your name. Line them up in order.
2. Younger kids can use 2x2 and 2x4 bricks and just line them up to form the letters of their name. You could also write the letters of their name on a piece of paper and they can trace it with the bricks.

Skills:
Spelling, Letter Recognition

Measuring Objects

Materials / Supplies

- 2x2 bricks or any other bricks

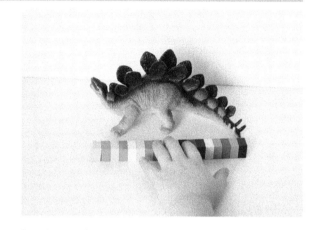

Instructions

While measuring with LEGO® bricks, young children are given an opportunity to practice measurement with a non-standard unit of measurement. Children will gain valuable counting practice when they count the number of bricks used to measure each object.

Children will practice estimation skills when making guesses about how many bricks long something is. Checking their estimates will help them to further develop more accurate estimation skills.

1. Stack the bricks on top of each other until they extend to both ends of the object you are measuring.
2. Count how many bricks long or tall the object is.
3. Compare the measurement of different objects. Which object is the longest? Which object is the shortest?

Extension: Estimate the length of an object. Now check your answer by measuring the object with bricks and then counting the bricks.

Skills:
Math

Bug Hotel

Materials / Supplies

- 4 square LEGO® baseplates
- Bricks in various sizes
- Good amount of 2x4 (or longer) LEGO® plates
- Natural materials to fill hotel

Instructions

1. Since LEGO® bricks can not connect to baseplates from the bottom, the floors of the bug hotel are designed to slide in and out like a pull out shelf. Start building from the bottom using 2x4 or longer plates with a 1x4 (or longer) brick in between with another 2x4 plate on top to create a slot to slide the baseplate in, creating the bottom. Build the slot to fit the sides and back of the square baseplate.
2. Build up the walls of the bug hotel about five bricks high on three sides.
3. Then repeat step 1 and insert another baseplate.
4. Repeat steps 1 and 2, two more times, or until you've reached the desired height of your bug hotel.
5. Once you have finished building the bug hotel, fill the compartments with sticks, twigs, grass and other yard clippings.
6. Set the bug hotel outside to encourage bugs to come stay in the hotel. Building a bug hotel is a great way to attract insects and spiders for science observation.

Skills:
Engineering

4 in a Row Game

Materials / Supplies

- 1x8 bricks
- 1/6 bricks
- 2x2 or 2x3 bricks in two different colors

Instructions

While playing this fun game, kids will practice critical thinking and strategizing. It is also a great way to work on social skills such as following directions, taking turns and being kind whether you win or lose.

1. Make a game board by placing 1x8 bricks end to end across a baseplate.
2. Use the 1x6 bricks to connect the rows above and below. This will make squares that you can put the game pieces in.
3. Use 2x2 or 2x4 bricks as game pieces. One color per person.
4. Each person will take a turns placing a game piece in one of the squares.
5. Players should start by placing a piece in one of the bottom squares of the game board. You cannot place a game piece in a square unless the square below it is already filled.
6. Players continue taking turns until one of them gets 4 in a row or all of the spaces are filled.

Skills:
Game Play, Critical Thinking

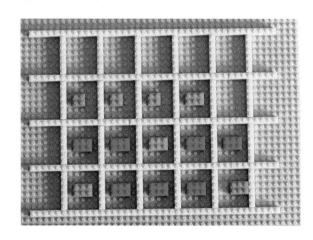

+ − Number Sentences

Materials / Supplies

- 2x2 bricks
- Paper
- Pencil/marker

Instructions

This is a hands-on way to illustrate addition and subtraction number sentences. The use of manipulatives gives children a concrete way to model abstract concepts and makes learning math more fun and engaging!

1. Write an addition number sentence with blanks for the numbers you are adding and the sum.
2. Use stacked 2x2 bricks to represent each number you are adding together and then invite your child to solve for the sum. They will create their own stack of bricks to represent the sum.
3. For more advanced learners, you can fill in the sum and one of the numbers being added and then have them solve for the blank number in the sentence.

Subtraction Instructions:
1. Write a subtraction number sentence with blanks for the numbers you are subtracting and the difference.
2. Use stacked 2x2 bricks to represent each number and then invite your child to solve for the difference. They will create their own stack of bricks to represent the difference.
3. For more advanced learners, you can fill in the difference and one of the numbers in the equation and then have them solve for the blank number in the sentence.

Skills:
Math

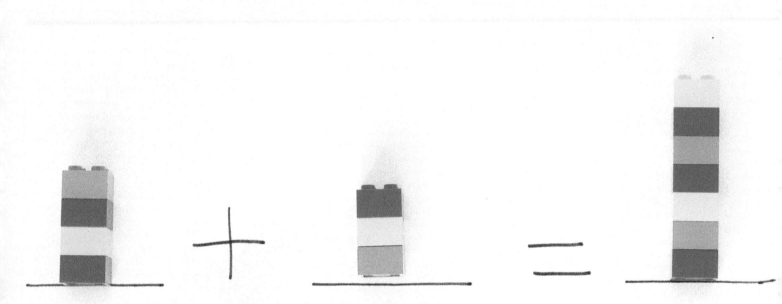

Ant Life Cycle

Materials / Supplies

- Green 32x32 stud baseplate
- 6 black 1x3 plates
- 2 black 2x3 plates
- 2 black 2x2 plates
- 1 black 2x3 slope brick
- 1 black 2x2 slope brick
- 1 1x2 plate with handle
- 2 black 1x2 plate with handle
- 8 black 1x1 plate with horizontal clip
- 1 black 2x1 plate with 2 horizontal clips
- 3 1x2 plates with handles on both ends
- 1 black 1x2 plate with low handles
- Tan 1x2 slope bricks
- White 2x2 slope bricks
- White 1x2 bricks
- 2x2 bricks
- 2x2 plates
- 2x4 or larger bricks for labels
- Printable labels
- Clear tape

Printable See Page 208

Instructions

1. Read about the ant life cycle in a book or on the internet.
2. Print out the labels and tape them to some extra bricks.
3. Then use the pieces to create ant eggs, ant larva, ant pupa and build an adult ant.
4. Label the ant life cycle using the correct terms.

Skills:
Science

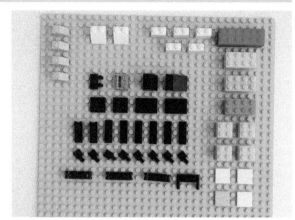

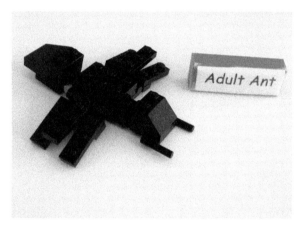

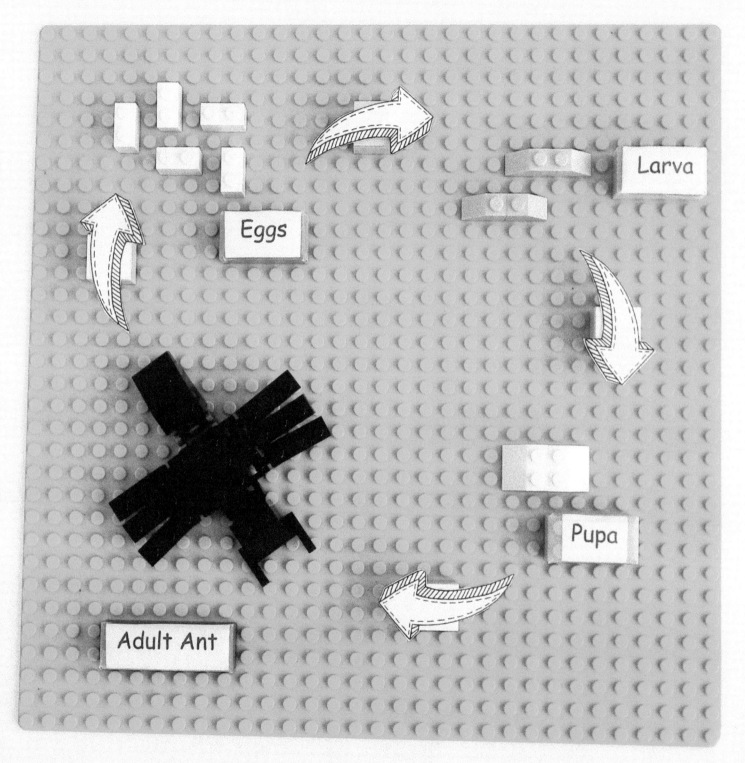

Eggs

Larva

Pupa

Adult Ant

19

Balancing Scale

Materials / Supplies

- 1 baseboard
- 2 12x2 plates
- 2 1x4 plates
- 1 gear element 2x2 double sided
- 8 2x2 bricks

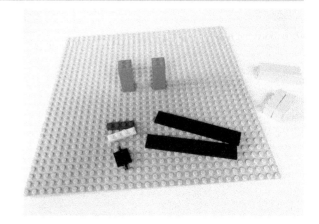

Instructions

1. Attach the 12x2 plates to each other by using the 2 1x4 plates underneath.
2. Attach the gear element to the center top.
3. Make a two 4 row high towers with 4 2x2 bricks.
4. Place them 3 studs apart in the center of the baseboard.
5. Balance the beam from step 2 upside down on the space between the studs of the tower.
6. Use random bricks to balance on either sides.
7. The goal of this activity to achieve balance.

Skills:
Logic, Engineering, Fine Motor

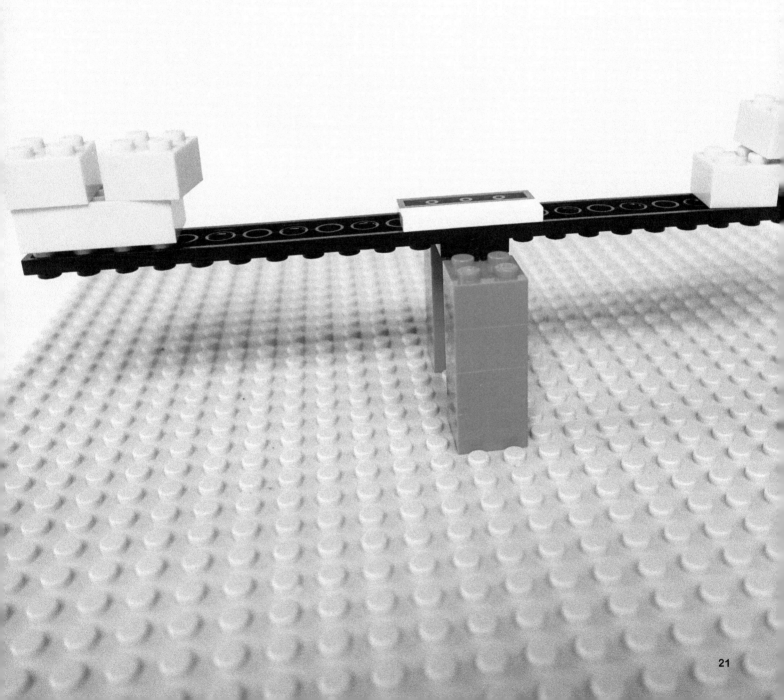

Multiplication with Arrays

Materials / Supplies

- 1x1 bricks (any color)
- Dice (optional)

Instructions

Multiplication can be a tricky subject for some children. Starting at a young age, visual and hands-on methods are a great way to make the learning concrete and form connections.

An array is a collection of objects displayed in rows and columns. They are useful representations of multiplication.

To make arrays with your child, ask them to make an array using simple multiplication problems such as 2x2, 1x4, 5x3, and so on. There is no need for formal "worksheets" or writing in the beginning. The goal is to allow children to understand the concept.

Once they are ready, you can have children roll 2 dice to depict a math problem they need to make in an array. For example if they roll a 2 and 4 they would make 2 rows of 4 bricks and their answer would be 8.

Skills:
Multiplication, Patterning, Visual Perception, Fine Motor

2 x 3

Birthday Cake Candle Counting

Materials / Supplies

- Pink, Tan and White bricks
- Round 1x1 bricks for candles
- Dice
- LEGO® numbers (see page 108) (optional)

Instructions

Children will learn number recognition and practice hands-on counting, addition or subtraction in a playful way with the LEGO® birthday cake and candles!

1. Build a cube with the bricks, making it look like a piece of cake. Use pink or white bricks in the center and top to represent frosting.
2. Build some birthday candles by stacking four to five round 1x1 bricks.
3. Playful learning with the birthday cake is fun, have children roll the number die, count out the LEGO® candles and stick them on the birthday cake. Alternately, children can roll a die and match up a number candle.
4. Create a larger birthday cake and more candles to practice addition and subtraction using two dice.

Skills:
Math

Bodies of Water

Materials / Supplies

- Blue bricks
- Green baseplate
- Printed labels
- Extra bricks for labels
- Scissors
- Tape

Printable
See Page
208

Instructions

Building bodies of water with LEGO® is a fun, hands-on way for kids to make connections with their geography and science lessons.

1. Print and cut out bodies of water labels.
2. Tape labels onto bricks and set aside.
3. Look up different bodies of water in a book or on the internet.
4. Use blue bricks to build various bodies of water on the green baseplate.
5. Label the bodies of water with the correct word.

Skills:
Science, Geography

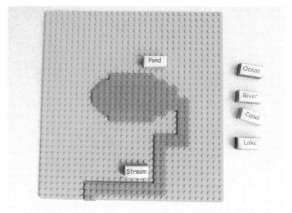

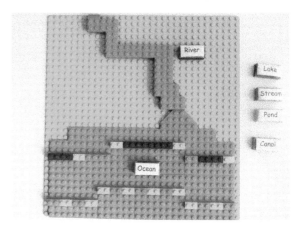

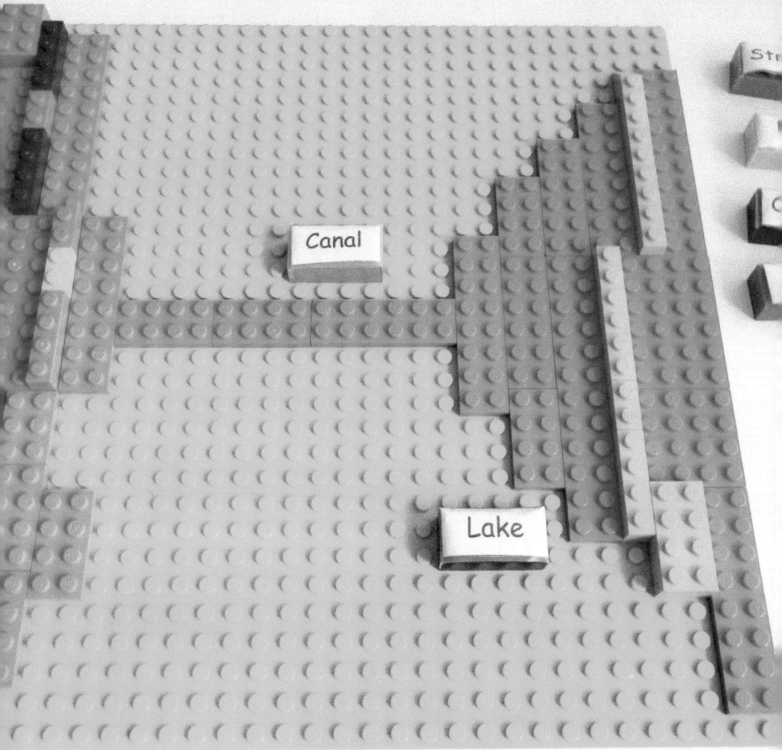

Canal

Lake

St

Bowling

Materials / Supplies

- Smallish ball that will fit in child's hand
- 45 2x2 bricks in various colors

Instructions

1. Create 9 bowling pins by making towers of 5 rows high each. Count as you make them.
2. Set these up on a flat surface with 5 in the back row, 3 in the middle row and 1 in the front.
3. Use the ball to bowl down the pins.

Skills:
Gross Motor, Aim

Brick-tionary

Materials / Supplies

- Permanent marker
- Enough matching bricks for all your words
- Access to a wide variety of bricks
- Dish or jar
- Rubbing alcohol to erase the marker at the end

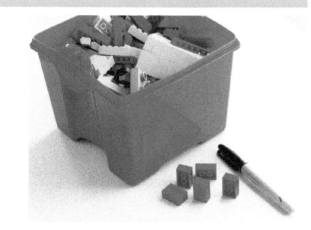

Instructions

1. Create a list of words that your child can read and could easily build from LEGO®.
2. Use your permanent marker to write one word one each of the matching bricks.
3. Place all the word bricks in a jar.
4. To play the game take turns picking a word brick out of the jar, not showing the other player. Build the item until the other person guesses what it is. You may wish to make rules such as: "the builder cannot give hints until after the item is fully built" or "the builder can only answer yes and no questions." Finding ways to describe the items will help your child's language abilities on both the hearing and the telling turns!

Skills:
Language

Build a Water Dam

Materials / Supplies

- Baseplate
- 2x2, 2x4, 2x6 bricks or assorted sizes of these in any color
- Connector pieces (2 sets). We used a 1x2 LEGO® plate with a handle on the side and a 1x2 LEGO® plate with horizontal clips. We added a 1x2 flat plate underneath the handle plate on each set.
- Container of water
- Tray or large container to place your project on to reduce mess. You can also take it outside.

Instructions

Can you stop the flow of water with LEGO® bricks? This is an interactive and fun activity that combines water play and learning! How does a dam work? Add a research component to the activity.

For an older kid, a great way to start this engineering project would be to draw a design! A good engineer starts with a plan. Young kids will certainly have fun building walls and exploring the water flow. You always have to test a design to make sure it works! Pour the water and see what happens. Do you need to fix anything? Can you build a better or different dam? Take it outside and set up a hose with a continuous flow of water. See if you can stop the flow!

1. Prop up the baseplate by building a wall out of 2x4 bricks or any combination of them. You can test out various heights. Our wall was 5 bricks high.
2. Put together your connector pieces. Add the 1x2 flat plate under the connect piece with the handle. I did find the base plate would not stay propped up. If you do not have connector pieces like these, use different ones. If you do not have connector pieces, use tape!
3. Build a dam! Use bricks to build a maze for the water. You can build areas for the water to pool, or you can build one large dam to stop the flow of the water at the very bottom of the plate.
4. Test your dam! Pour a cup of water slowly through your project. Are there any leaks? You can go back and tweak your design and repeat the process over and over again.

Skills:
Engineering

Building Sight Words

Materials / Supplies

- 1x4 bricks
- Chalk marker or dry-erase marker

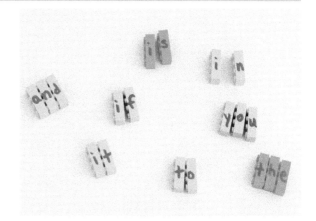

Instructions

This is a fun, hands-on approach, to teaching kids sight words. You can do this with any words you would like your kids to learn how to spell.

1. Decide which sight words you want to use.
2. With a chalk or dry-erase marker, write each letter of each word on a separate 1x4 brick turned sideways as shown in the pictures. Make sure they are all turned the same way.
3. For younger kids, you may want to include a list of all the words that need to be built.
4. Put all of the pieces in a pile on the table.
5. Invite your child to put the bricks together to form sight words.

Skills:
Spelling

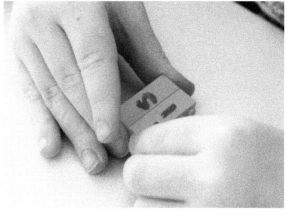

Cloud Diagrams

Materials / Supplies

- Large gray baseplate
- White bricks in various sizes
- Gray bricks in various shades and sizes
- Yellow bricks
- Blue round 1 plates
- Various 2x4 or larger bricks for labels
- Printed cloud labels
- Scissors
- Clear tape

Printable
See Page
208

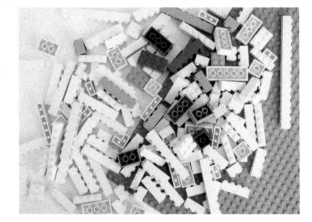

Instructions

Building a cloud diagram with bricks is a wonderful hands-on activity for a science lesson. It's a great way for kids to solidify knowledge and understanding of clouds.

1. Print out cloud labels and gather supplies.
2. Cut out labels and tape to 2x4 or larger bricks.
3. Look up different cloud formations in a book or on internet.
4. Use white and gray bricks to build cloud diagrams on gray baseplate.
5. Label the clouds using correct terms.

Skills:
Science

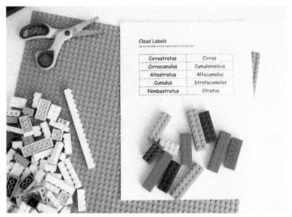

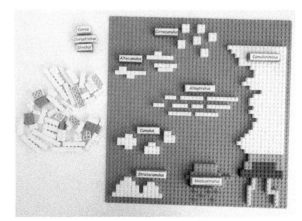

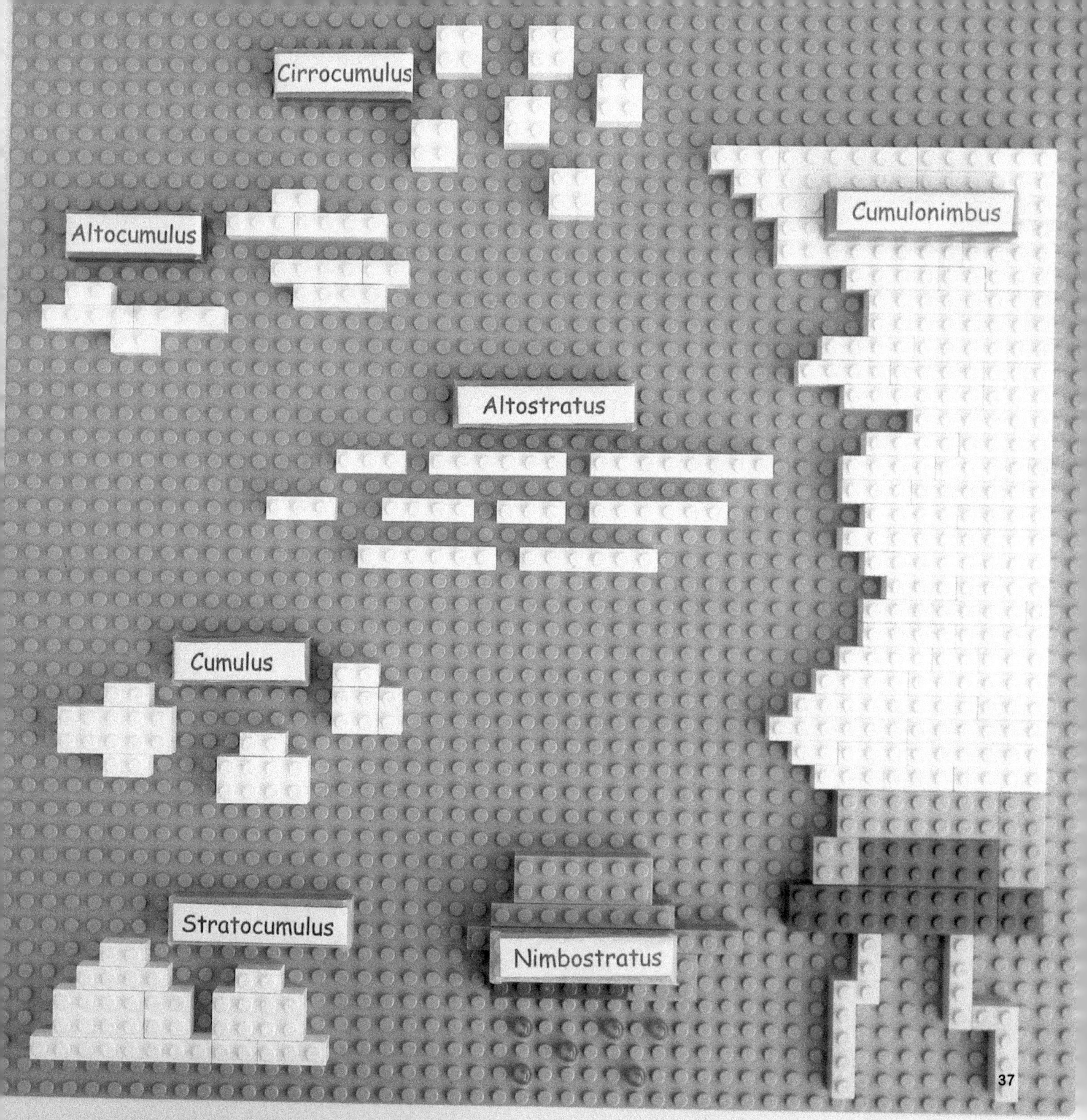

Cirrocumulus

Cumulonimbus

Altocumulus

Altostratus

Cumulus

Stratocumulus

Nimbostratus

Color Slots

Materials / Supplies

- 1 16x6 plate
- 76 2x1 bricks
- 6 1x4 bricks
- 6 2x1 flat plates
- 6 red 2x2 bricks
- 6 blue 2x2 bricks
- 6 green 2x2 bricks
- 6 yellow 2x2 bricks
- 6 pink 2x2 bricks
- Assortment of bricks

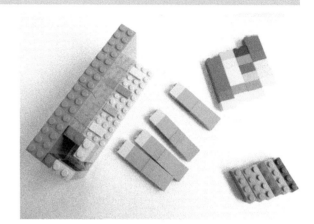

Instructions

1. Make eleven 6 row high towers with 2x1 bricks.
2. Line 5 of the towers on the first row of studs of the plate, leaving a one stud gap, turn the 6th tower to stay on the plate.
3. Line up 5 more towers to make an L shape as shown in the image.
4. Add a 2x1 or 2x2 flat plate to the area inside the L (this is to stop the 2x2 bricks attaching).
5. Complete the back wall of the slots with random bricks to make it close.
6. Use the 6 1x4 bricks to secure your towers to the wall.
7. Complete by using 10 2x1 bricks to finish off.
8. Slot each color 2x2 brick into the grooves to color stack.

Skills:
Fine Motor, Color Sorting

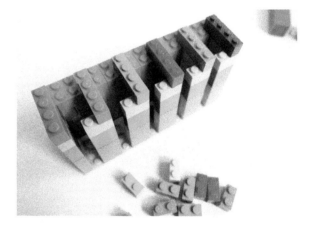

Color Sort and Build

Materials / Supplies

- About 10-20 bricks of any size bricks in 5 or more colors

Instructions

This is a great way to introduce children to color names. While putting the bricks into separate piles, children will learn to sort objects. Sorting is a beginning math skill. As children build structures, they are developing fine motor skills while exercising their small hand muscles.

1. Put all of the bricks in a pile.
2. The child will sort the bricks into smaller piles by color.
3. Then they should build a structure with each color.
4. If you use bricks of varying sizes, children can sort the objects by size instead of color.

Skills:
Fine Motor, Math

Colors and Counting Game

Materials / Supplies

- 2x4 bricks in 6 different colors. You will need about 10-15 of each color.
- A baseplate
- Minifigures to use as game pieces
- Dice

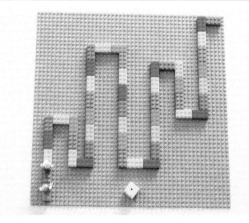

Instructions

While playing this color game, children will practice identifying colors by name. They will also practice counting and one to one correspondence while moving their game pieces across the game board.

1. Place the 2x4 bricks end to end all around the baseplate so that they travel up and and down and side to side across it.
2. Place the minifigures on the table right in front of the starting brick.
3. Players will take turns rolling the game die and moving their minifigure that many spaces on the board.
4. Once a player lands on a space, they should call out the color they landed on.
5. Players take turns until one of them reaches the end of the game board.

Skills:
Color Recognition

Create a Maze

Materials / Supplies

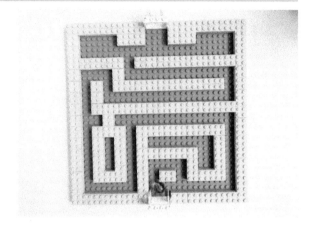

- 1 baseplate
- Many bricks in the same color or various colors
- 1 marble
- 2 windows

Instructions

1. Place the windows at opposite ends of the baseboard.
2. Build the other area of your maze to contain the activity.
3. Build a maze like structure inside the baseboard leaving 2 or 3 studs open for the marble to fit in (this all depends on the size of your marble, it is best to measure).
4. Once completed the challenge is to get the marble from one window door to the other with either fingers or by lifting the baseboard up and tilting it to move to the end.

Skills:
Fine Motor, Puzzle Solving, Dexterity

Cars City Maze

Materials / Supplies

- 2x2 bricks
- 2x4 bricks
- Cars

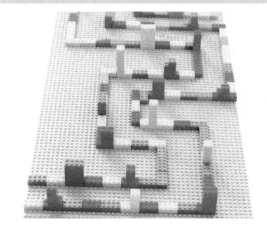

Instructions

While playing, children will use critical thinking skills to get through the maze. This will also help to develop eye-hand coordination. When playing with other kids, it is also a great way to develop vocabulary and social skills like sharing and taking turns.

1. Use the 2x4 bricks to make a maze that goes around the length of two baseplates. Make sure the spacing of the maze is wide enough to fit a small car.
2. Use the 2x2 and 2x4 bricks to build small towers and stores along the edges of the maze.
3. Drive small cars through the maze. You can go back and forth each way too!

Skills:
Critical Thinking, Social Skills

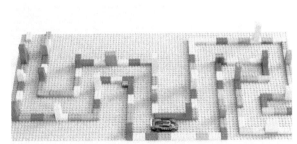

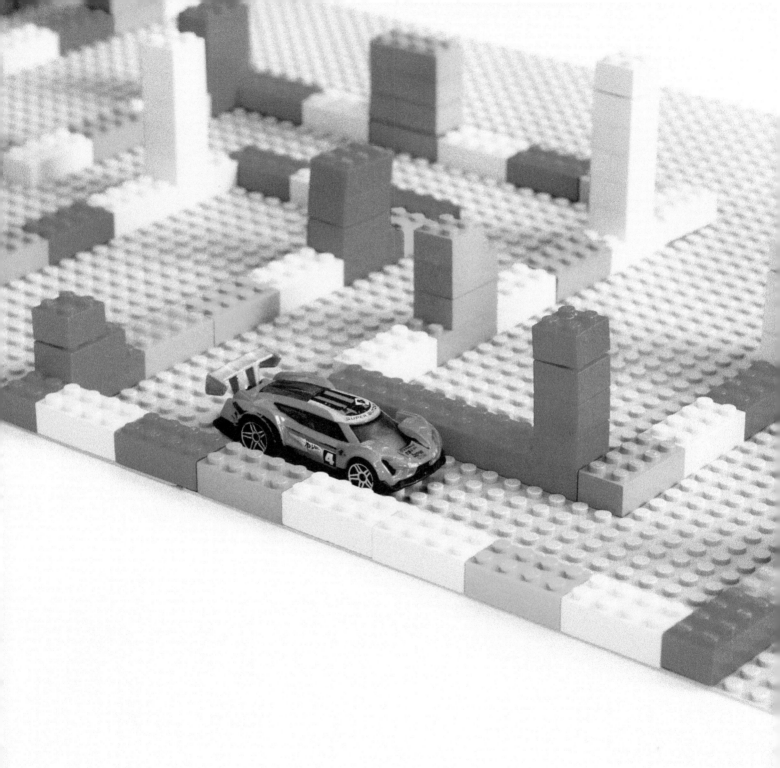

Duplo Paint Machine

Materials / Supplies

- Duplo turntable brick
- 2x2 Duplo bricks
- 2x8 Duplo plate
- 4x8 Duplo plate
- Paintbrush
- Tempera paint
- Paint tray
- Large sheets of white paper
- Blue sticky tack

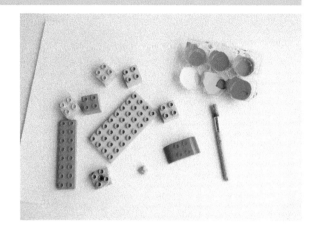

Instructions

Building and painting with a Duplo Paint Machine is a wonderful way for kids to experiment with science, technology, engineering, art and math (S.T.E.A.M.).

1. Use bricks, plates and turntable to build a paint machine. Make sure it is the correct height to fit your paintbrush.
2. Use the blue sticky tack to attach the paintbrush to the bottom of the 2x8 Duplo plate and to keep the paint machine upright by sticking some to the bottom of the 4x8 Duplo plate.
3. Dip the paintbrush in the paint, attach the paintbrush to the paint machine.
4. Place paint machine on top of large sheet of white paper and spin it around to paint circles on the paper.
5. Experiment with using the paint machine with different paint colors, building and painting with the paint machine at different heights, and spinning the machine fast and slow.

Skills:
S.T.E.A.M.

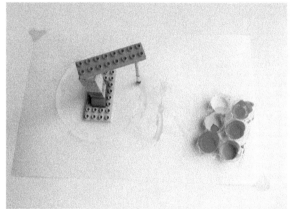

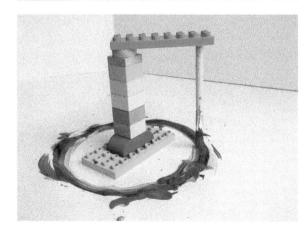

Duplo Pendulum Painting

Materials / Supplies

- Duplo bricks and plates
- Duplo hook brick
- Duplo baseplate
- Large sheet of white paper
- Plastic or styrofoam cup
- String
- Tempera paint (watered down)

Instructions

Duplo pendulum painting is not only a neat process art project, but also a fun way to demonstrate gravity for a science lesson!

1. Poke a hole in the bottom the cup and under the rim on either side to tie the string.
2. Thread the string through the top holes in the cup, creating a long handle.
3. Using the Duplo bricks and plates, build a structure to hang the pendulum from.
4. Place a sheet of white paper under the hanging pendulum.
5. Fill your pendulum cup with some watered down tempera paint and give the cup a push!
6. Watch the paint drip out of the cup, creating a neat pattern as the pendulum swings.

Skills:
Art, Science

Duplo Stamps

Materials / Supplies

- Variety of Duplo bricks
- Tempera paint
- Large sheet of white paper
- Paint tray
- Large sponge brush
- Tape

Instructions

This Duplo activity works really well for toddlers and young preschoolers. Exploring creativity as well as colors and shapes is a foundation of early learning.

1. Use Duplo bricks to build stamps in various shapes and sizes (2x2 bricks can be used as a handle for the stamps).
2. Spread out a large sheet of white paper on a table or flat surface. Use tape to hold it in place.
3. Set out a tray of tempera paint and the Duplo bricks. Invite children to create with the stamps.

Skills:
Colors, Shapes

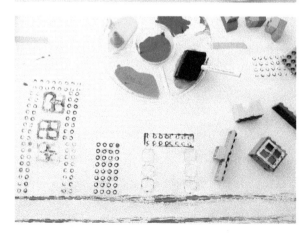

Exploring 2D and 3D Shapes

Materials / Supplies

- Play dough
- Cube: 6 2X4 bricks
- Rectangular solid: 2 2X8 bricks, 4 2X4 bricks, 4 2X3 bricks and 2 2X2 bricks
- Pyramid: 6 2X3 bricks, 2 2X4 bricks and 1 2X2 brick
- Wedge: assorted bricks 2 studs wide stacked to form wedge
- Cylinder: 1 cylinder shaped piece, if available
- Play dough rolling pin (optional)

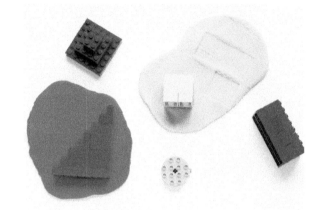

Instructions

1. Construct the 3D shapes. Use this step as a build challenge for your child and allow them to create the shapes or recreate these as follows:
Cube: Lay out 2 2X4 bricks next to each other, stack 2 more in the opposite direction on top of those. Finish by stacking the remaining 2 2X4 bricks across the top in the opposite direction.
Rectangular solid: Start by laying out 2 2X8 bricks out next to each other. Add the 4 2X4 bricks across the tops of them to hold them together. Finish by adding the 4 2X3 bricks and the 2 2X2 bricks to the top.
2. Roll out your play dough flat. Take turns pressing the various sides of the 3D shapes into the dough and talk about the 2D shapes that are created.

Skills:
Shapes

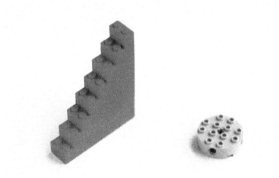

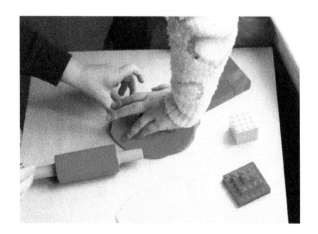

Fine Motor Transfer Game

Materials / Supplies

- 2x2 bricks
- 2 small bowls
- A spoon
- Children's tweezers
- Stopwatch or timer

Instructions

While playing this game, children will get lots of valuable fine motor practice that exercises and develops their small hand muscles and increases fine motor control. Depending on how you play, it can also be a fun way to practice counting!

1. Put the 2x2 bricks in a small bowl and set it on the table.
2. Place an empty bowl next to it and lay a spoon or tweezers nearby as well.
3. Kids will use the spoon or the tweezers to transfer the bricks from one bowl to another. I have found that the spoon is easier for toddlers and preschoolers. The tweezers are better for older preschoolers and young kids.
4. There are two ways you can play the game. You can use a stopwatch to record how long it took to transfer the bricks from one bowl to the other and the fastest time wins. Or for some added counting practice, you can use a timer set to a certain amount of time and the person who transfers the most bricks in that amount of time wins.

Skills:
Fine Motor, Counting

Geoboard

Materials / Supplies

- 9 bearing element 2X2, single
- 9 wide rims (tires removed)
- 3 10x2 plates
- 6 2x2 plates
- 9 1x2 plates
- Assortment of 2x2, 3x2 and 4x2 bricks in your chosen color
- Small rubber bands

Instructions

1. Attach the wide rims to the bearing elements.
2. Attach 3 of the tireless wheels to a 10x2 plate with a spacing of 2 studs between them.
3. Fill in the gaps on the 10x2 plate with 2x2 plates and 2x1 plates.
4. Repeat steps 1-3 two more times, you want a total of 3.
5. Attach bricks to the front and back of the rim assembly to cover the plates.
6. Use additional bricks to pad between two of the assemblies to provide an equal spacing for geoboard use.
7. Stretch out the rubber bands between the rims of your new LEGO® geoboard.

Skills:
Hand Strength, Fine Motor

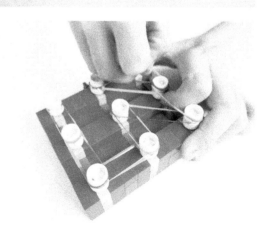

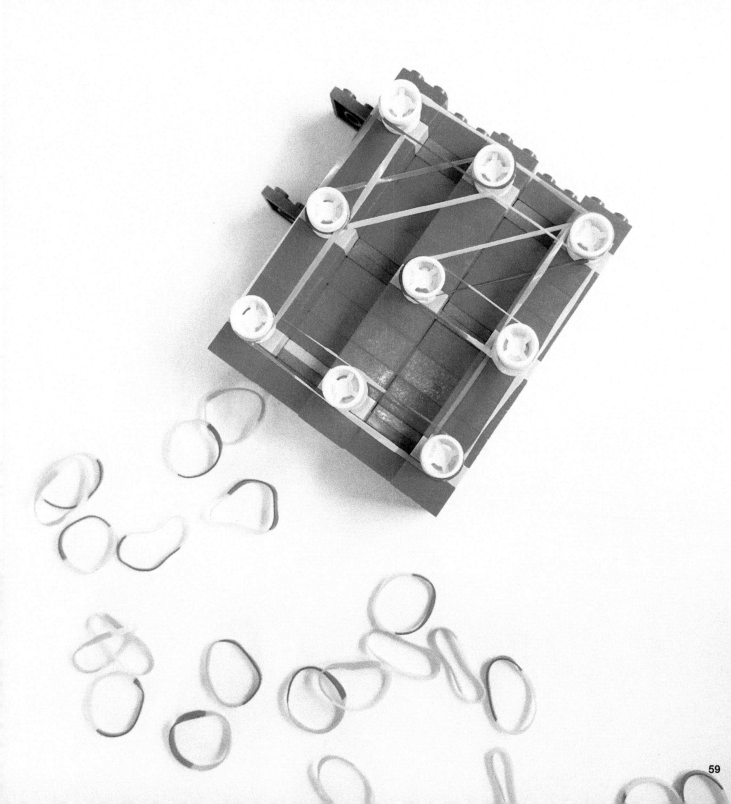

Graphing by Color

Materials / Supplies

- 2x4 bricks in various colors
- Paper
- Ruler/straight edge
- Crayons/markers

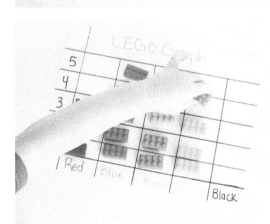

Instructions

Children will learn how to read data on a simple graph. They will also practice counting, color recognition, sorting, and comparing amounts.

1. Make a graph on the paper with markers and a ruler.
2. For children who can't read yet, write the color names with a marker of the same color. This will make it possible for them to identify the colors they are graphing.
3. Place a different amount of each color brick in a single pile.
4. Invite your child to sort the bricks and place them on the graph accordingly.
5. Talk about the data the graph displays.
    * How many _____ (insert color) bricks were there?
    * Which color had the most bricks?
    * Which color had the least bricks?
    * Did any colors have the same amount of bricks?

Skills:
Math

LEGO Graph

Blue   Green   Yellow   Bl

Hand Counting

Materials / Supplies

- Large baseplate
- Various bricks that are 2 studs wide, the bigger the better, and all the same color if you have enough matching bricks
- Dice (optional)

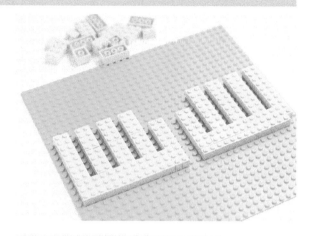

Instructions

1. Start constructing the hands by laying out the fingers. Place one 2X8 brick or two 2X4 bricks, one stud away from the left side edge. This will be the left pinky finger. Place the remaining fingers of the left hand one stud apart.
2. Repeat on the right side for the other hand, again using either 2X8 bricks or 2X4 bricks.
3. Fill in the bricks of the palm of the hand with the remaining bricks.
4. Once the hands are complete you can use them for counting. You can either use them only for pointing, or you can "fold down" the fingers for counting.
5. Use your fingers for counting practice, making tens, addition or subtraction, as desired. You can add a game die, rolling and counting that many fingers, or bricks with numbers written on them, for addition and subtraction.

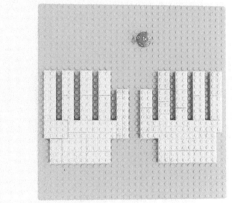

Skills:
Math

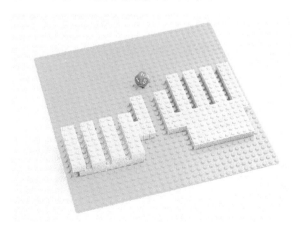

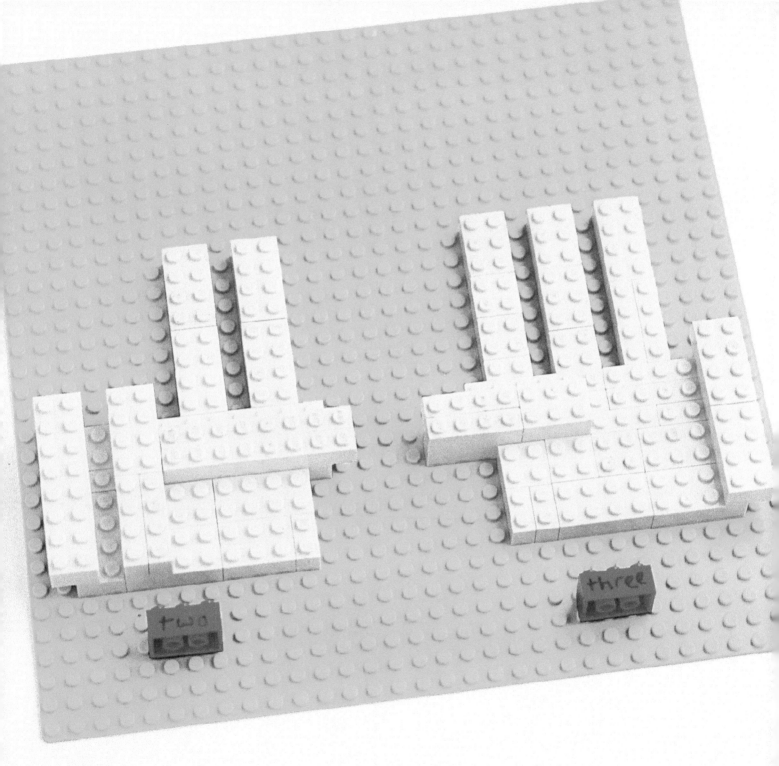

Hidden Memory Game

Materials / Supplies

- 60 2x2 bricks in base color
- 6 pairs of 2x2 bricks in various colors

Instructions

1. Arrange 4 2x2 base color bricks in a square.
2. Connect them by adding a 5th 2x2 brick on top in the middle.
3. Add a 2x2 color brick underneath this assembly.
4. Repeat steps 1-3 to complete 12 of these items.
5. Layout the memory units in a grid of 4x4.
6. To play the game turn over 2 units at a time to find the matching colors.

Skills:
Logic, Memory

Insect Anatomy

Materials / Supplies

- 32x32 baseplate
- Black or brown bricks in variety of shapes and sizes (including 1x2 bricks, 1x4 bricks, 2x4 bricks, 2x3 bricks, 2x8 bricks, 1x2 slope bricks, 1x3 slope bricks)
- Extra bricks for labels
- Printed labels
- Scissors
- Clear tape

**Printable
See Page
208**

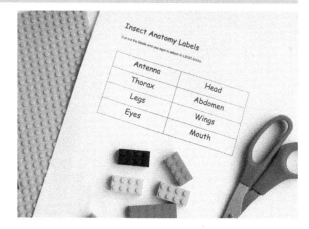

Instructions

Building and labeling an insect with LEGO® is a great hands-on activity to add to a science unit about insects.

1. Print, cut out, and tape insect anatomy labels to extra bricks.
2. Read about insect anatomy in a book or on the internet.
3. Using the bricks listed above, have child(ren) build an insect on the baseplate.
4. Then label the parts of the insect body using correct terms.

Skills:
Science

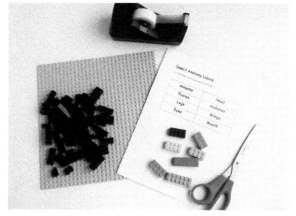

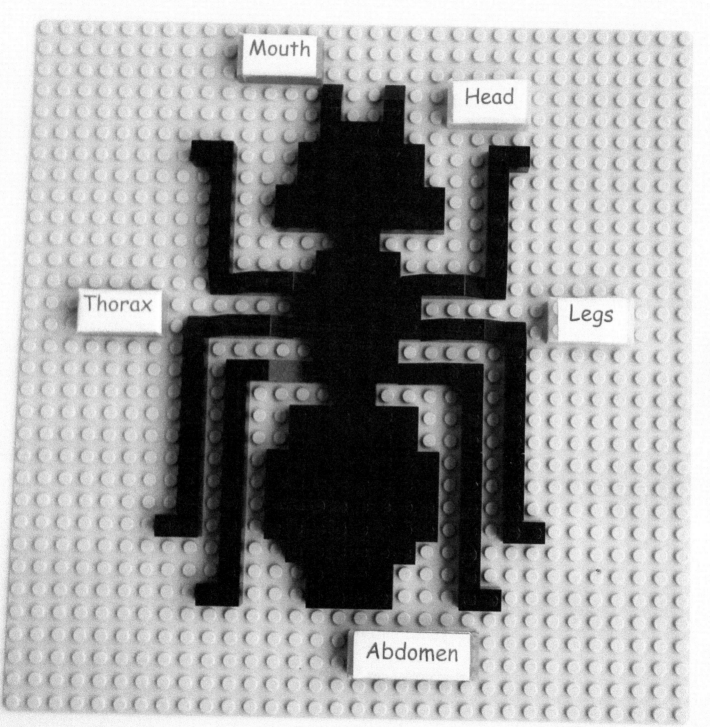

Learning Place Value

Materials / Supplies

- 2x2 bricks
- Small pieces of paper
- Marker or other writing tool

Instructions

This is an excellent way to visualize and model the place value relationships of numbers. Understanding place value lays the groundwork for regrouping in addition, subtraction, multiplication, and division.

1. Write each number on a small sheet of paper or an index card.
2. Talk to your child about how the first number represents the tens place and the second number represents the ones place.
3. Count out 10 bricks and stack them. Repeat this as many times as you need to based on which numbers are being modeled. These stacks represent the tens.
4. The loose 2x2 bricks represent the ones. If you are modeling the number 16 you will have one ten stack and 6 loose ones bricks. If you are modeling the number 25, you will have two tens and 5 ones.

Skills:
Math

+ - Part Part Whole Method

Materials / Supplies

- A Variety of Flat LEGO® Pieces (combinations that equal the same size, for example 2 2x2s equal 1 2x4)
- Part Part Whole Play Mat

Printable See Page 208

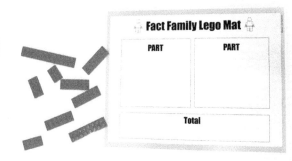

Instructions

Part Part Whole (PPW) method is a math concept involving the relationship between 2 or more parts. For this activity, you will encourage your child to create combinations and find the missing pieces in any new combination.

For example, place a 2x6 flat LEGO® in each "Part" and ask your child to find a LEGO® flat that represents the "whole". They would find the 2x12 and place it in the whole section.

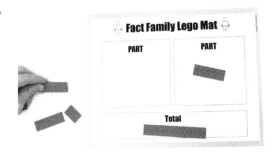

Another way to use PPW, is to place a large flat in the whole box and have your child make a combination that relates. For example, if you put a 2x8 in the whole box, they could use a 2x4 plus a 2x4 OR a 2x6 plus a 2x2.

Finally, in order to practice early subtraction, fill only two of the boxes (one part and the whole) and have your child find the missing piece.

There are so many variations to this game. Once your child has the concrete examples down, they can move to more abstract examples using just the numbers.

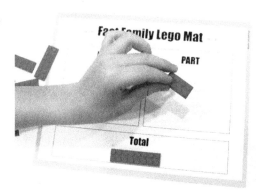

Skills:
Counting, Simple Addition, Simple Subtraction, Problem Solving

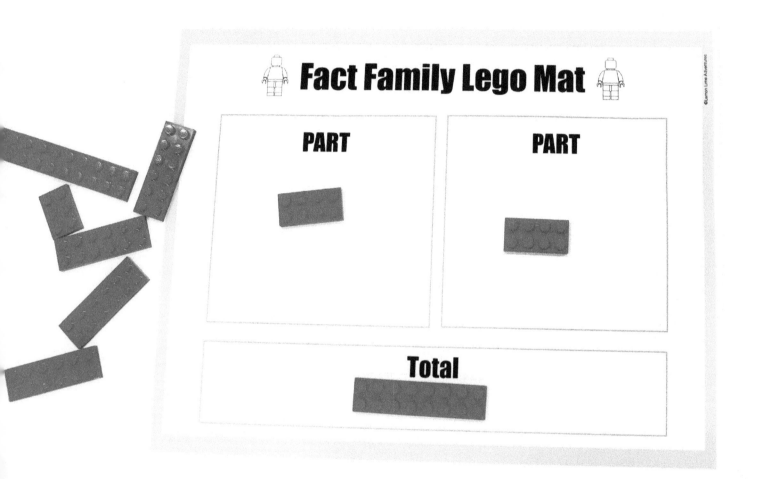

Fact Family Lego Mat

PART	PART

Total

Alphabet

Materials / Supplies

- Bricks (2x2, 2x3, 2x4)

Instructions

The challenge is to build a model for every letter of the alphabet. The pictures shown are a great example, however it is important to encourage your child to think about the shapes and lines of a letter before they begin building.

Each child will see the letters a little differently and build them with different pieces, which is part of the fun. If you are struggling to get started, begin with letters that have all straight lines such as L, E, F, T, etc.

Once all of your letters are made, they make great displays or even manipulatives for language arts games. You can put them in alphabetical order, match upper and lower case, sort by types of lines in each letter, sort vowels and consonants, and even spell words... the possibilities are endless.

Skills:
Letter Recognition, Fine Motor, Early Reading, Early Spelling

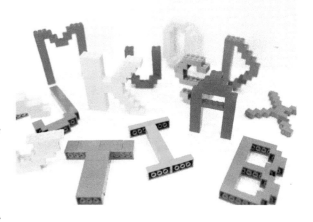

Straw Construction

Materials / Supplies

- Various bricks that are 2 studs wide, the longer the better
- Drinking straws
- Small baseplates

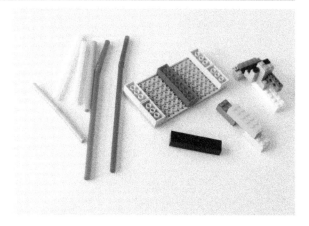

Instructions

1. Trim the drinking straws to various lengths. Make sure some match each other.
2. Attach several bricks to the bottom of the small baseplate and lay the baseplate upside-down on the work surface.
3. Show your child how the straws can stick onto the round parts of the bottom of the bricks.

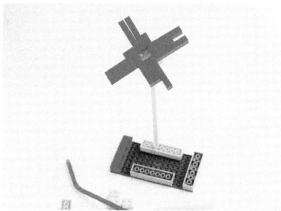

Skills:
Engineering, Fine Motor

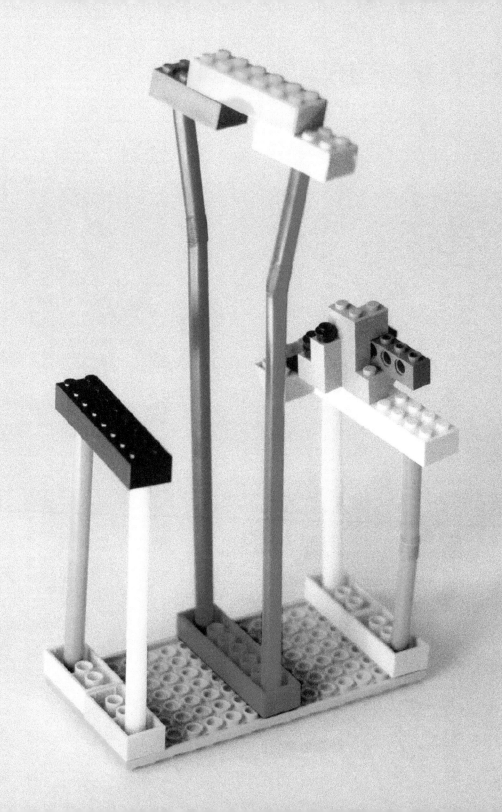

Art & Symmetry

Materials / Supplies

- Plates in various sizes and colors including one solid color to make a dividing line
- Baseplate of any size

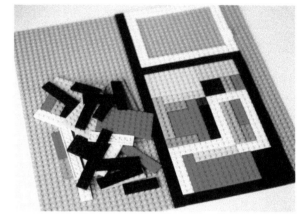

Instructions

This type of symmetry is called reflection symmetry. The line of symmetry can be top to bottom or left to right. When the second half is complete it will be a mirror image of the first half. Not a copy. The image is flipped around the line of symmetry producing a mirror image. You may need to demonstrate this by starting the activity. Work from the center out. If you do not have enough plates, you can also use various size bricks.

Symmetry is an excellent math activity including geometry. Plus you can produce beautiful art. We often see symmetry in art, nature, and architecture. You can also explore other types of symmetry with LEGO® including point symmetry and rotational symmetry.

1. Divide the baseplate in half using all one color plate. We chose black. This is called the line of symmetry.
2. Create a design or pattern on one half of the baseplate. Make sure you have the pieces to be able to complete the other half!
3. Set out the pieces for the other half and the baseplate.
4. Encourage your kids to have fun exploring symmetry.

Skills:
Symmetry

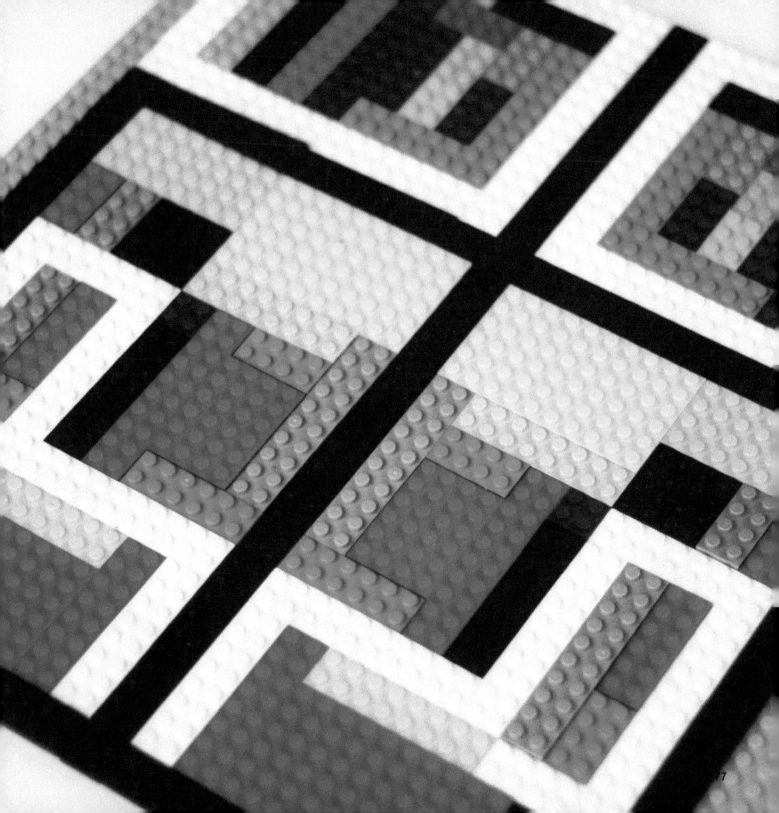

Balloon Cars

Materials / Supplies

- Balloons
- LEGO® car parts including wheels, plates, bricks, steering wheels, and other fun pieces to build cars.
- LEGO® tiles 1x2 with handles (this is where balloon is inserted)
- Painters tape to make lines (optional)
- Measuring tape to measure distance (optional)

Instructions

Test out your engineering skills and experiment with the power of air pressure! What happens when you blow up a balloon and let it go? The air comes rushing out of it and the balloon is propelled forward. That is exactly what we are doing with this balloon powered LEGO® car! For every action, there is an equal and opposite reaction.

When the air comes rushing out of the balloon attached to your car, it will propel your car forward. Hopefully in a straight line! Ours did not always go straight. What factors would affect that? Play around with the shape and size of your LEGO® car. What if you blow up the balloon more, less? Does that affect the car?

Add math to the activity by measuring the distance your car traveled. Keep a log and try the same car a few times to see if the number is pretty accurate. You can also make a game out of it and race your friends! Who will build the faster LEGO® car?

1. Build a car from the car pieces you have gathered. Go ahead and try out a few different sizes. We had different sets of wheels to try out.
2. You can make each car the same and just change one thing like we changed the wheels. Or you can make each car unique!
3. To attach the balloon, we used a 1x2 flat with a handle. You can get creative if you don't have one and make something similar.
4. Push the balloon through so that the opening so the balloon is pointing away from the car. What happens if the balloon is facing the wrong way?
5. Go ahead and make racing lines with the painter's tape if you want, but it is totally optional.

Skills:
Engineering, Math

Boats Experiment

Materials / Supplies

- Empty shallow dish
- Water
- Pennies
- Bricks (any variety)

Instructions

Challenge your child to build a boat that can hold the most pennies. They can use any variety of LEGO® and any design.

1. Fill a shallow dish with enough water for your boats to float.
2. Place each boat in the water and add pennies to your boat one at a time until the boats start to sink.
3. Count how many pennies your boat could hold.
4. Once you have tested two boats, challenge your child to alter their models to hold more pennies.

Skills:
Science, Math, Fine Motor, Problem Solving, Engineering

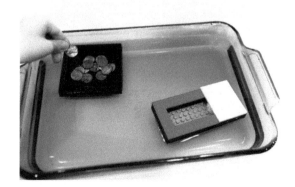

Bridge Building Activity

Materials / Supplies

- Baseplate (we chose blue to represent water)
- Assorted bricks, small plates, and flats
- Minifigures to test the bridges
- Measuring tape (optional)

Instructions

Be a Civil Engineer for the day. Plan, design, and build your own bridges. This LEGO® bridge building activity is a terrific STEM challenge for kids. There is plenty of opportunity to use science, technology, engineering, and math skills to prepare, design, build, problem solve, and test the strength of the bridges!

Older kids can look up pictures of different bridges to build more complicated designs. Younger kids may just enjoy simple bridge building with plenty of minifigure play afterwards. Why not build a boat?

1. Build mounds of land on either side of the plate. We started with 4 2x4 bricks to make a square two bricks high.
2. As you work your way down the baseplate add a 2x4 brick to the mounds so that the distance between the mounds gets shorter. Refer to our set up for ideas.
3. Set out a variety of bricks, small plates, and flats for your kids to use.
4. Make sure to have minifigures available to test the bridges!
5. Encourage your kids to find creative ways to make bridges between the mounds.

Skills:
STEM

Bubble Wands

Materials / Supplies

- Assorted bricks - ideally 8-10 2X3 bricks for the handle, 2 2X8 bricks and 6 1X2 bricks. Also, if available, use bricks with holes in them.
- Bubble solution
- Shallow dish or recycled plastic lid

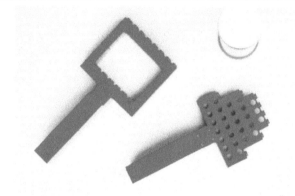

Instructions

1. Build your bubble wands. Make the building part of the challenge by seeing who can make the best bubble wand or directly recreate the ones shown here:
Frame wand: Build a rectangle using 2 2X8 bricks at the top and bottom and sides made of 3 1X2 bricks. Place one 2X3 brick at the bottom of the rectangle, then build a tower of 2X3 bricks and attach those to it, offset by one stud.
Holes wand: Stack several bricks with holes in them to form a wall of holes. Add one 2X3 brick to the bottom, then build a tower of 2X3 bricks and attach those to it, offset by one stud.
2. Pour bubble solution into a shallow dish, dip the wands into the solution and blow bubbles.
3. Talk about what properties help to make a good bubble wand. What other features can you try?

Skills:
Engineering

Car STEM Challenge

Materials / Supplies

- Bricks (any variety)
- Wooden block or cardboard

Instructions

1. Challenge your child to build 3 identical cars out of LEGO®. They can use any variety of bricks and any design.
2. If your child needs help, guide them to look at the cars we have here for a sample.
3. If your child is young, they can use pre-made LEGO® cars and change the wheels.
4. To properly test variables, all the cars should be identical except one thing (the size, the wheels, the weight, etc).
5. After making a ramp out of small blocks or cardboard, have your children race the cars to see which one is the fastest.

Skills:
Science, Math, Problem Solving, Engineering

Catapult STEM Challenge

Materials / Supplies

- Bricks (any variety, we used a combination of longs, flats, and technic pieces)
- Rubber bands
- Small toys to toss

Instructions

Challenge your child to build a catapult out of LEGO®. They can use any variety of bricks and any design.

If your child needs help, guide them to build a base first, adding on arms and the moving parts last.

There are two kinds of catapults your child can attempt. One uses force, while the other uses the tension of a rubber band.

How many different ways can your child engineer a catapult? Which design shoots the farthest? Can they measure how far it launches?

Skills:
Science, Math, Fine Motor, Problem Solving, Engineering

Challenge Cards

Materials / Supplies

- LEGO® Challenge Cards (in printables section)
- Scissors
- Laminator and pouches (optional)
- Access to various bricks

Printable
See Page
208

Instructions

1. Cut out the LEGO® Challenge Cards and laminate, if desired.
2. Show your child how to pick a card, read it and then complete the challenge.
3. Variations: Make it a two player game and see who can complete their challenge first. Make it a cooperative, turn taking experience by completing the challenge together, adding one brick per turn.

Skills:
Engineering, Visual and Spatial Planning

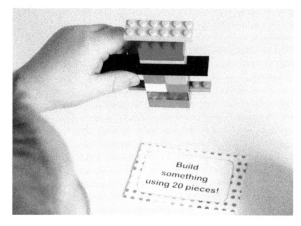

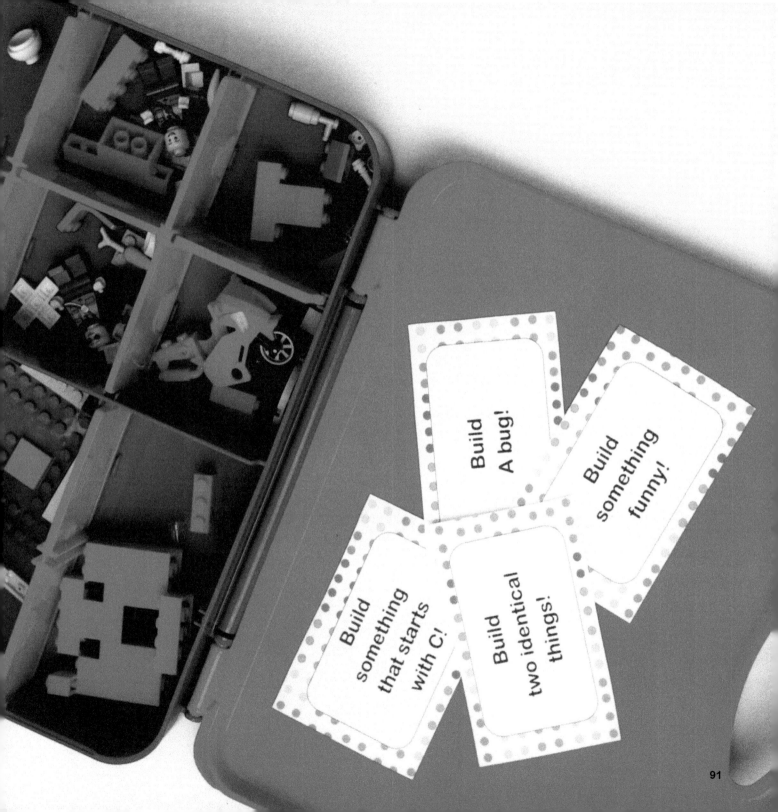

Build
A bug!

Build
something
funny!

Build
something
that starts
with C!

Build
two identical
things!

Combinations of Ten

Materials / Supplies

- 10 of your child's favorite minifigures
- Pencil
- Combinations of Ten Free printable

Printable
See Page
208

Instructions

This activity is meant as a beginning lesson to demonstrate why the math facts that combine to make the number 10 work. Often times children are asked to memorize the combinations but lack the understanding of why the numbers go together.

Start with 10 minifigures on one side of the play mat and slowly move a character to the other "team". Each time your child moves a minifigure, record how many are in each set.

Skills:
Counting, Simple Addition to Ten, Writing Numbers to Ten

Displacement Experiment

Materials / Supplies

- 2 measured containers of water
- Bricks (we used 2×2 and 3×2)

Optional:
- Ruler
- Measuring cups

Instructions

1. Fill two glasses with water to the same level. Place your pile of bricks next to the glass and invite your children to participate.
2. Before you begin, chat with your kids about the level of the water. You can show them examples of displacement using ice cubes and water, or you can let them discover it on their own. Talk about what they predict will happen when they put the bricks in the glass and how many bricks they think they will need to change the level of the water.
3. As you drop the bricks in one at a time, keep track of the total (we love to tally ours up to practice a little more math).
4. The challenge is to change the water level without adding any more water to the container.
5. Try different bricks in the other container and compare the changes.

Note: When you use an item such as LEGO® that float, noticing the change in the water level can be a little difficult. If your children are very young, I would suggest using items that sink (LEGO® wheels work perfect).

Skills:
Science, Math, Fine Motor

Emotions Station

Materials / Supplies

- Assorted bricks in colors that represent emotions:
- Red=Anger
- Blue=Sadness
- Yellow=Joy
- Green=Disgust
- Purple=Fear
- Assorted small bricks for facial features
- Large baseplate

Instructions

1. Start by talking about different emotions. You may wish to watch Disney Pixar's Inside Out to spark discussion.

2. One-by-one, build the different emotions with your children. You can make your own version or copy these:

Anger: Build a square that is 2 studs deep, 8 studs wide and 6 bricks tall. Include 1X2 black bricks for eyes and a small black window for the mouth. You may wish to alternate orange 1X2 bricks on the top. Add a red base to the bottom and fire pieces to the top if available.

Fear: Construct a question mark shape using 6 2X4 purple bricks and 2 1X4 purple bricks. Use a white 2X4 brick to make the "blank space" between the top of the mark and a round purple piece at the bottom.

Joy: Construct a happy face made from yellow bricks, red for the mouth and blue for the eyes. Add a yellow base and an exciting flourish at the top by snapping a flat 2X3 brick between the studs on the top brick.

Sadness: Construct a tear shaped sad face using various blue bricks. If clear or blue tinted clear bricks are available, use those for the eyes.

Disgust: Construct a disgusting looking figure using various green bricks. Add flower stems without the flowers for extra yuck factor.

3. Attach your emotions to your base plate and any time your child is feeling big emotions he or she can go to the emotions station to identify what he or she is feeling. Use this as a tool to label feelings and work through big emotions.

Skills:
Emotion, Social Situations

Excavation

Materials / Supplies

- Ice cube tray or large ice block mold
- Water
- Salt
- Toothpicks
- Minifigures

Instructions

1. To prep your frozen minifigure, fill an ice mold halfway with water and place a minifigure in the middle of the mold. Allow 2 hours to set, and then fill the rest of the way until the mold is completely frozen with the minifigure stuck inside.
2. Give your child the challenge to be an archeologists that needs to excavate the fragile fossilized minifigure from the ice. Provide them with water, basters, toothpicks, and salt.
3. Help your child notice the changes in the ice, the ice crystals forming, and the amount of water they see. Ask questions about why they think this is happening. What could they do to speed up the process?

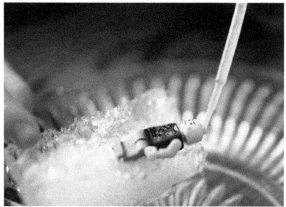

Skills:
Science, Verbal Skills (Asking and Answering Questions), Fine Motor, Sensory Integration (Tactile and Proprioceptive)

Hearts

Materials / Supplies

- Bricks 2x2, 2x3, 2x4, 2x6 (any combination) in a variety of colors

Instructions

These LEGO® hearts use basic bricks making it easy for all LEGO® fans to build! When putting together hearts, your child will have the opportunity to practice counting skills as well as problem solving skills. Based on the bricks you have available, your child will determine what combination of bricks will complete the heart. An example would be if you did not have a red 2x4 brick available, you can substitute it with (2) 2x2 red bricks. Similarly if you have a longer brick, you can use less of the smaller bricks.

Your child will also have the opportunity to work on visual skills as he or she copies the pattern of rows in the heart. You can even connect the hearts together lying flat or connect them vertically for an added challenge to test engineering skills!

1. Choose the brick colors for your heart. You can use any combination of colors!
2. Start with a 2x2 brick for the bottom of the heart.
3. Add 5 rows each longer than the next with a 1x2 overhang off each level.
4. The 7th row is either a 2x4 or (2) 2x2 bricks. These bricks are placed one space in from the edge from either side. A 2x2 gap should be in between both sections.
5. The last row is a 2x2 brick placed in the middle of each of the (2) 2x4 sections.

Skills:
Counting, Problem Solving

I Spy Bottle

Materials / Supplies

- Large plastic water bottle. This one is a voss water bottle, but any plastic bottle will work.
- Small LEGO® pieces including 1 stud bricks, minifigure heads, and minifigure accessories such as hats, tools, animals, glasses, telescopes, mugs, snowshoes, crystals or jewels, or whatever else you have!
- Rice to put in the bottle. (Other fillers such as sand, dried beans, or small pasta works well, too)
- Funnel (optional but helps to transfer filler to bottle)

Instructions

I spy bottles are great for developing literacy skills, visual processing skills, and patience. Add in pre-writing skills if you have your kids circle, check or cross out items on a list.

I used our tablet to take a picture of the items in the I spy bottle. No need to print anything! Makes a perfect on the go activity for restaurants or long car rides. You can, of course, take a photo of the items and print out a copy to go with the bottle.

Alternatively, you can write out the items in the bottle for older kids and even kids who are learning how to sound out letters and recognize color words. Adding items like hats and bricks in a variety of colors is great practice for early reading.

An I spy bottle is a great quiet time or independent learning activity, but it can also be used for parents and kids to work together.

1. Start with a clean, dry, plastic bottle.
2. Alternate adding items and rice so they are dispersed as evenly as possibly throughout the bottle.
3. Do not fill completely. Fill only about 2/3 of the way up the bottle so the items have room to move around.
4. Put the cap on and tighten it. You can use tape to seal the bottle but still allow you to open it later to remove items.

Skills:
Literacy, Visual Processing, Pre-writing

Light Up Candle

Materials / Supplies

- 1x6 bricks for tall candle
- 1x2, 1x3, 1x4, 1x5, or any combination of these for square candle
- Square plate at least 8 stud by 8 stud to fit tealight for square candle
- Battery operated tealights for both candles

Instructions

Plan, design, and build your own LEGO® light up creation. Using a simple battery powered tealight, you can create a candle, nightlight, mini-lantern, and so much more. A LEGO® light up project is a great way to incorporate a bit of technology into your LEGO® learning time. It is also a terrific way to use counting, patterning, and problem solving to build a practical light source for your room. Test out different size candles as an experiment to see what size, shape, and design is the best. Draw designs first and keep a journal of your creations!
There are two variations of our light up LEGO® candle idea. Feel free to use your imagination and try out your own design.

1. To make the tall candle, alternate 1x6 bricks in the pattern shown in the picture. Each row will line up with previous rows in an alternating pattern. make your candle as tall as you like! This does not have a plate on the bottom. Place over tea light for a light up LEGO® candle.

2. To make the square candle, start with a plate at least 8 studs x 8 studs. Vary the rows of 1x2, 1x3, 1x4, and 1x5 bricks to create openings. Make sure to alternate where the openings are placed as you build your candle. Place tea light inside. Since this one has a base, you can move it from room to room.

Skills:
Engineering

Memory Game

Materials / Supplies

- Printable memory card pieces
- Card stock
- Superhero minifigures (optional)

Printable
See Page
208

Instructions

After you have printed the memory game, you are ready for hours of fun for all ages. There are 4 super fun ways to play this game (and even more if you let your kids get creative and imaginative with it).

4 Fun Ways to Play:
1. For Toddlers or Preschool: Place all the cards face up on the table or floor. Each player takes a turn to find a match. Matches can be big to little, character to vehicle, or character to character.
2. For Early Learners: Place only pictures face down on the table. Each player takes turns trying to find a match.
3. For Any Age Learner: Place one set of pictures and one set of words/names down on the table and have the players try to match the picture with the title.
4. For Advanced Learners: Place two sets of words/names down on the table and have players match the cards.

Skills:
Cognitive Skills, Verbal Skills, Visual Matching, Early Reading

Numbers

Materials / Supplies

- 2x2, 2x4, 2x6 bricks in a variety of colors (alternatively any mix of 2x2 or 1x2 bricks can be used)

Instructions

Use LEGO® numbers to explore math in a hands-on way. You can also build a plus sign, a minus sign, and an equal sign to practice addition and subtraction. Note that I did use small plates to make the math signs.

With our LEGO® numbers we can practice number recognition and simple addition or subtraction problems. Kids can build their own math problems and solve them!

For the younger kid, you can also use 2x2 bricks to go along with the numbers for one-to-one correspondence. You can also use the 2x2 bricks to help solve addition and subtraction problems.

1. Gather as many bricks as you can! You are going to need quite a few to make all the numbers. Hint: You can also use 1x2, 1x4, and so forth so build your letters and to mix in with the 2x2 style bricks.
2. Check out the sample numbers and use them as a guide to build your numbers.
3. You decide the height, length, and width. Use your imagination and get creative.

Skills:
Math

Obstacle Course

Materials / Supplies

- Various bricks
- Various flat pieces
- Various small baseplates
- Various triangle/wing pieces

Instructions

1. Construct various obstacles. Use this portion as a build challenge or recreate the ones shown:

Arrows: If you have triangle type wing pieces, attach 2 wing pieces to a long flat piece to create an arrow. Construct a tower of 2X4 or 2X3 bricks and snap the long flat piece of the arrow between the studs of the tower. Check for balance as you may need to adjust.

If you do not have wing pieces you can use flat pieces to construct arrows. At the end of one long flat piece, attach a flat 2X2 brick. Right next to it, attach a flat 2X4 piece and finally add a 2X8 next to that. Construct a tower of 2X4 or 2X3 bricks and snap the long flat piece of the arrow between the studs of the tower. Check for balance as you may need to adjust.

Green hurdle: Snap a small flat green baseplate in between the studs of another small flat baseplate to create a hurdle.

Wall hurdle: You can also construct a low, wide wall to use as a hurdle.

2. Set them up in a line with enough space to run around the arrows and jump over the hurdles. Run the obstacle course, rearranging the obstacles as desired.
3. This obstacle course also works great with LEGO® vehicles and other toys for some pretend play fun!

Skills:
Gross Motor Skills, Engineering

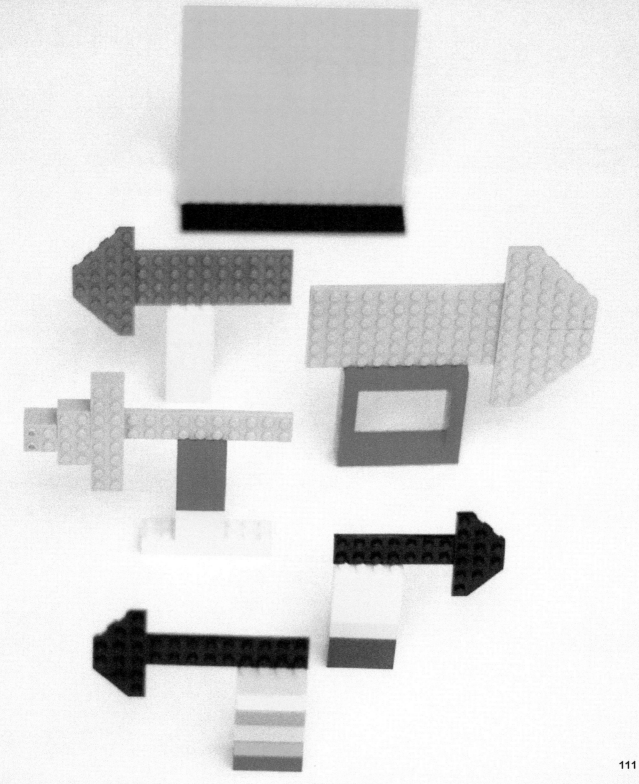

Play Mat Design

Materials / Supplies

- Poster board
- Markers, crayons, or colored pencils
- Craft tape and scissors (optional)
- Miscellaneous craft supplies or construction paper (optional)
- LEGO® pieces, minifigures, and accessories

Instructions

Be an urban planner. Designing is fun! Plan out a city, a construction site, a playground, an island, or whatever you can imagine. A mat is a fun way to add a new play element to your LEGO®.

Making your own play mat involves tons of great fine motor skills. Drawing lines and shapes for where buildings or water will be placed is great for pre-writing skills. Using scissors to cut tape or construction paper is also great for skills practice. This can become a very involved project that opens the door to great storytelling. Build LEGO® creations to go along with your design.

1. Set out a large piece of white poster board.
2. Set out markers, crayons, colored pencils, or other drawing materials.
3. Use a marker to draw roads and other interesting areas on the poster board. We included a lake, a construction site, a small pond, and an airplane landing strip.
4. Color your play mat. Use craft tape if desired to decorate or outline areas. Our landing strip was made with silver and red craft tape.
5. Add LEGO® creations. We built a house, a police station, a dock for the boat, and a water tower. We also added some of our LEGO® city vehicles.

Skills:
Engineering, Fine Motor

Pom Pom Blow Maze

Materials / Supplies

- Large baseplate
- Large assortment of bricks that are 2 studs wide
- Straw
- Pom pom

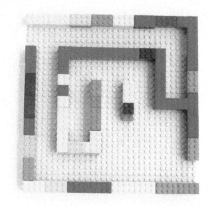

Instructions

1. Begin by constructing a wall that is 2 bricks tall and 2 bricks wide all the way around the outside of your baseplate, except for two openings that are 4 studs wide each.
2. Construct inner maze walls leaving a path that is 4 studs wide.
3. Place the pom pom at one opening and take turns using the straw to blow the pom pom through the maze.
4. You and your child can take turns creating new and different mazes.

Skills:
Oral Motor Skills, Engineering

Reading Aids

Materials / Supplies

- For the minifigure pointer:
- 1 LEGO® Minifigure
- 1 straw or craft stick

For the line isolating pointer / finger pointer:
- 7 1X8 bricks (same color)
- 4 1x2 bricks (same color)

Instructions

1. For the Minifigure Pointer: Cut the straw in half, pinch one end closed and insert it between the minifigure's legs. A craft stick may be used instead.
2. For the Line Isolating Pointer: Stack five 1X8 bricks together, then separately stack the remaining two 1X8 bricks together. Make two towers of two 1X2 bricks. Add one of the small towers to each side on the top of the larger 1X8 section. Add the smaller 1X8 section on top of the two 1X2 towers.
3. For the Finger Pointer: Stack all seven 1X8 bricks together. Stack all the 1X2 bricks together. Place the 1X2 bricks tower on top of the 1X8 tower to resemble a pointing hand.
4. Show your child how to use the pointers to help follow along while reading any text.

Skills:
Literacy

I like to build with

my favorite thing to play

...e to play with my LEGO tru...

...een.

Seasons Mosaic

Materials / Supplies

- Large baseplate. I chose blue to represent the sky but any color will work.
- Flat pieces in a variety of sizes and colors that will work for trees, leaves, clouds, sun, grass, and snow.
- Single stud pieces for leaves, buds, raindrops, and snowflakes in a variety of colors.
- 1x2, 1x4, 1x6 black bricks to divide the base plate into 4 sections. Any color will do, but using the same color will divide the spaces better.

Instructions

Use this fun seasons activity to explore the different seasons. Create each quadrant with a specific ground cover, tree, and sky that is most associated with the season. You can give it depth by stacking flats and using varying shades of one color such as two different greens for the grass or different shades of grey for the rain clouds.

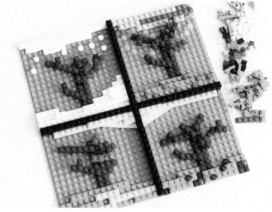

Continue to learn about each season by checking out books related to the seasons. You can use books to recreate a specific scene in a book. Practice writing skills by writing a descriptive sentence or two about your seasons board. You could also add a sentence or two about activities you like to do or what the weather feels like!

1. Determine the best way to divide your baseplate into four even sections. They may not be exactly even. Use any combination of the 1x2, 1x4, and 1x6 bricks to make the dividers.
2. Use our model to give you inspiration.
3. Start by adding the ground covering. Determine what type of ground covering is most relevant to each season.
4. Add a basic tree to each scene. We went through and tried to recreate the same simple tree in each section. Depending on how many brown flats you have, you might have to change up your tree designs.
5. Add your leaves and buds depending on the season.
6. Create sky or specific weather that is appropriate for the season. Our model is just one idea. Have fun and try out different ones with your seasons.
7. Don't forget to add precipitation too.

Skills:
Seasons

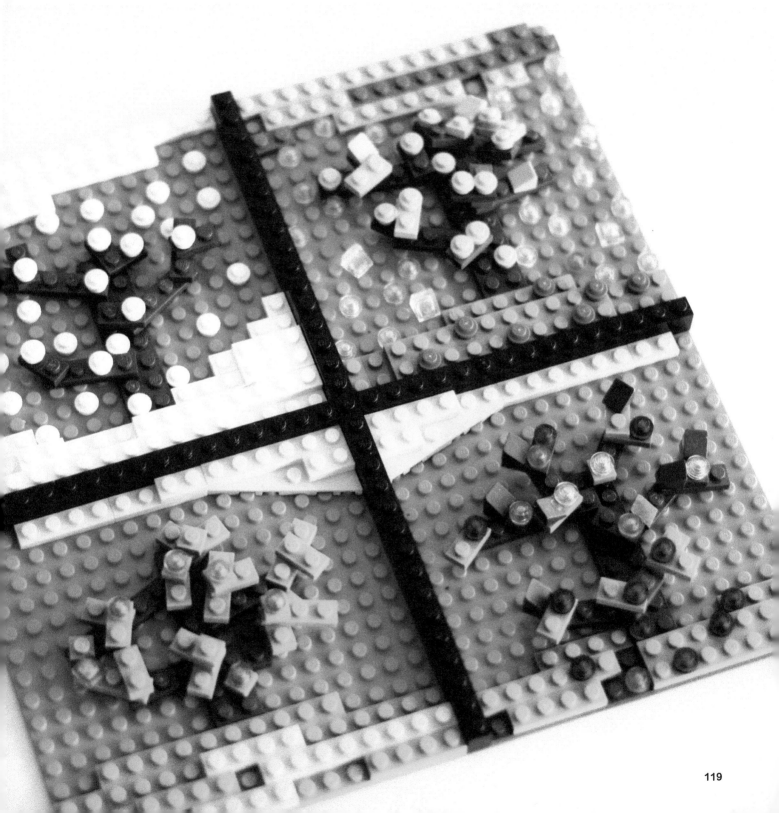

119

Sensory Bins

Materials / Supplies

- LEGO® (any variety)
- LEGO® minifigures (optional)
- Rice
- Large shallow container

Instructions

1. Sensory bins are a great opportunity to explore the senses while playing with a favorite toy. The set up is simple but the possibilities are endless.
2. Start by filling a large shallow container with rice. Then choose your scene or goal for your sensory bin. We chose to make ours a shipwrecked junk yard.
3. You can fill yours with certain colors, shapes, accessories or whatever your heart desires and turn it into an I spy game.

Skills:
Sensory Input, Fine Motor, Pretend Play

Shadow Puppets

Materials / Supplies

- Minifigures
- Assorted bricks
- Craft sticks or drinking straws
- Flashlight

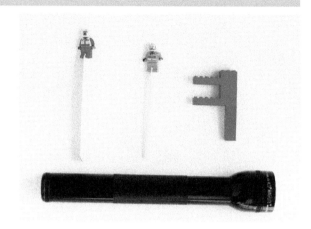

Instructions

1. Insert craft sticks or a pinched drinking straw between the legs of your minifigures (trim the straw, if desired).
2. Build any other shadow puppets, as desired. Build your own or build the alligator head that we built as follows: Create a handle by stacking up a tower of 1X2 bricks. On top of the tower add a 1X8 brick. For a closed mouth add another 1X8 brick. For an open mouth add two 1X3 or 2X3 bricks on top of the 1X8 brick, then add another 1X8 brick for the top of the mouth. Finish him off with a 1X3 or 2X3 brick for the eyes.
3. Find a dark room, turn on your flashlight and take turns making stories with your shadow puppets.

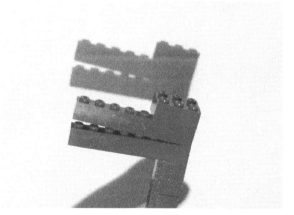

Skills:
Language, Storytelling

123

Slime

Materials / Supplies

- 2 bottles of clear glue
- 1/2 cup liquid starch
- Various small LEGO® pieces (such as studs, heads, accessories)

Instructions

1. Pour both bottles of glue into a small bowl and slowly add in the liquid starch while stirring constantly.
2. Mix until well formed and a slime consistency you prefer.
3. Add in small LEGO® pieces.

Variations: You can add in small 1x1 bricks with letters or numbers written on them for older children.

Skills:
Fine Motor, Measurement, Counting, Sensory Integration (Tactile and Proprioceptive)

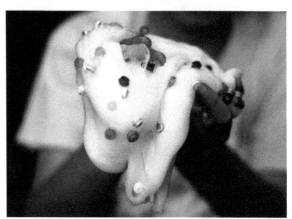

Stamped DIY Cards

Materials / Supplies

- Premade LEGO® Hearts (You can turn to page ... to get instructions for making hearts)
- Red paint
- Card stock paper

Instructions

1. Start by creating hearts the size you desire. Then use 2x2 bricks to make a handle on the back.
2. Carefully dip the heart stamp into red paint and wipe off any excess paint.
3. Slowly place your stamp on a folded piece of cardstock paper.

Get creative with the size of the stamps you make and the placement. Anyone would be lucky to get a card like this!

Skills:
Art, Fine Motor, Sensory Integration (Tactile)

Ten Frame Game

Materials / Supplies

- Various bricks that are 1 stud wide
- 10 2X2 bricks in 2 different colors (for a total of 20)
- Large baseplate
- Dice (we used a 12-sided one and a 6-sided one, but 10-sided die would be great too)

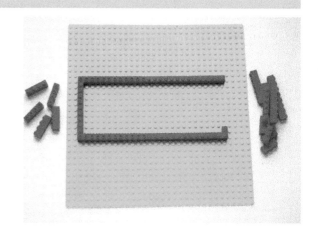

Instructions

1. Construct your ten frame. Using any combination of 1X1, 1X2, 1X3, 1X4 or 1X anything bricks, construct the outside rectangle of your ten frame. Next place the 4 bricks to divide the rectangle frame into 5 tall spaces. Finish by adding the small bricks to divide each of the 5 spaces into two.

2. Separate your 2X2 counter pieces so that each player has one color.

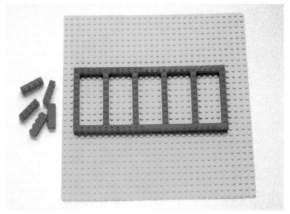

3. Play the game. Roll the die. One person fills in that number of spaces with the counters. The other person needs to fill in the rest of the spaces to make ten. If you are using a die with numbers over 10, those numbers count as roll again. Switch and let the other person go first, continue taking turns as desired.

Skills:
Math

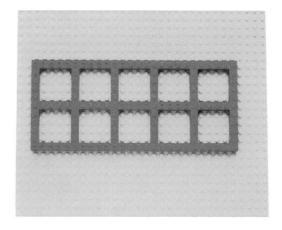

Tennis Ball STEM Challenge

Materials / Supplies

- Tennis ball
- 12" ruler
- Large baseplate
- Several small plates (more for young kids, less for older kids)
- Assorted bricks

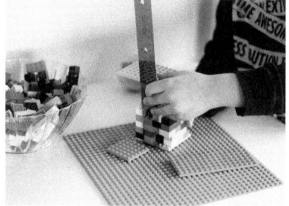

Instructions

LEGO® is awesome for engineering skills. This activity also involves using a ruler to measure the tower as progress is made. Older kids can use a yardstick for an additional challenge. Plan carefully to use the resources you have to build a tower tall enough, stable enough, and sturdy enough to hold the tennis ball and meet the height requirement.

Additionally, the amount of plates and bricks you leave out can also be part of the challenge. Younger kids can have free access to LEGO® pieces. Older kids can have the added challenge of only being allowed a certain number of small plates.

Will you take the challenge? Don't get discouraged if it takes a few times to build the right tower. It's a great learning process along the way.

1. Set out bricks, plates, tennis ball, and ruler.
2. Explain the challenge. Use the plates and bricks provided to build a tower 12 inches tall that can hold a tennis ball up on the very top.
3. Let the kids build, measure, plan, and problem solve.

Skills:
Engineering

Tessellation Puzzle

Materials / Supplies

- Bricks in 2x2 and 2x4 or a combination of these sizes in a variety of colors
- Alternatively 1x2 and 1x4 bricks can be used
- Use additional size bricks as needed

Instructions

Tessellation is a math activity. It is also a puzzle and goes beyond simple patterning. Tessellation is the tiling of geometric shapes without gaps. It is usually the same shape repeated over and over again across a flat surface.

It also becomes a simple puzzle and art design idea making it a fun STEAM project. It may be best to make each shape it's own color but have fun with whatever brick colors you have. Multiple ages can enjoy this activity together by building simple shapes or more complex shapes depending on ability. Can you create a different set of shapes that will repeat without gaps or spaces between them?

1. Build one simple shape that can easily be repeated and interlocked with one another. We built this C shape.
2. To build this C shape, I pushed 2 2x4 bricks together. Try to use all one color per shape.
3. Add 1 2x2 brick under the ends of step 2.
4. Connect all the bricks together with a second layer of bricks. This is where you can also use 1x2 and 1x4 bricks if you don't have enough.
5. Make as many as you can.
6. Get creative and come up with new shapes that will also work.

Skills:
Math

133

Tic-Tac-Toe

Materials / Supplies

- Minifigures
- Plates of various sizes or a baseplate
- Tiles of various lengths that are 1x or bricks that are 1x

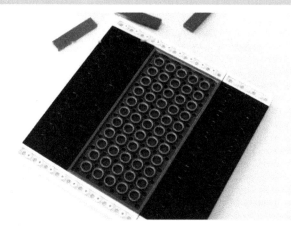

Instructions

There are several great learning ideas here with this simple LEGO® tic-tac-toe game. Planning the board, gathering the right pieces, and building the tic-tac-toe pattern is a terrific opportunity to use visual, math, engineering, and fine motor skills.

Two person games teach social skills, sharing, turn taking, and good sportsmanship. Plus, you can have fun choosing minifigures and redesigning the board with your teammates.

Toss this LEGO® tic-tac-toe game into a bag and you have a great travel activity too.

1. Build the tic-tac-toe board using thin plates or a baseplate. Our small tic-tac-toe board is made using a 14 stud square that we created from a combination of different sized plates. It is double level so that all the pieces are firmly connected. We also made one on a 32 stud baseplate.
2. Add either a combination of 1x tiles (flat smooth pieces) or 1x bricks to make the dividers on the tic-tac-toe board. On our 14 stud board, on every 5th stud I placed the tile. You can use a combination of tile lengths to make the dividers.
3. Gather your minifigures into two distinct teams. My son chose boys versus girls. We have also used pirates versus skeletons. Alternatively, you can use regular bricks for game pieces.

Skills:
Engineering, Game Play

Truck Load Math

Materials / Supplies

Parking lot game board:
- 1 large baseplate
- 6 1X6 bricks
- 4 1X4 bricks

2 trucks:
- 4 sets of 2 wheels
- 2 2X6 flat pieces
- 8 2X2 pieces
- 2 window pieces (optional)

Math symbols:
- 2 2X8 flat pieces (preferably black)
- Other various bricks to act as truck load materials (aka counters), 1X1 bricks are the best
- Container to hold the load/counter bricks

Instructions

1. Create the truck parking spots on the baseplate using 3 1X6 bricks and 2 1X4 bricks for each one. The two parking spots are made with three sides of a rectangle, as shown.
2. Create the trucks by stacking two 2X2 bricks onto each set of wheels. Connect two sets of wheels onto each of the 2X6 flat pieces. Add the window bricks or 2X2 bricks to the front of the trucks.
3. Show your child how to make the greater than, less than, and equals symbols with the two black 2X8 pieces and describe what they mean.
4. Take turns loading up counter blocks onto the back of your trucks and parking them in the parking spots. Use the black math symbol pieces to show if one is greater than, less than, or if they are equal.

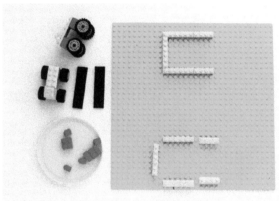

Skills:
Math

Volcano

Materials / Supplies

- Large baseplate
- Bricks in various sizes and colors (we chose black, brown, and grey)
- Plastic 8 oz water bottle
- Baking soda
- Vinegar
- Liquid food coloring (reused red and yellow for orange lava)
- Container for vinegar (into volcano)
- Dish soap (optional)
- Large, shallow plastic storage bin, lid, or tray (used to contain the mess)

Instructions

A LEGO® volcano is an awesome science experiment with ordinary kitchen ingredients. When baking soda and vinegar combine, they make a chemical reaction. This happens when an acid and a base mix. In this case the acid is the vinegar and the base is the baking soda. Together they form carbon dioxide which is the eruption. You can feel the fizzing, bubbling reaction. The size and shape of the bottle help to push the liquid up and out like a volcano erupting. If you add dish soap, you get a foamier eruption. It's definitely fun either way. Kids love baking soda eruptions!

1. Place the water bottle in the middle of your baseplate.
2. Use your LEGO® bricks to build up a volcano around the bottle. Check out our volcano for inspiration. Place the volcano into a shallow container or on tray to contain any mess.
3. Add a few tablespoons of baking soda to the bottle.
4. Add food coloring to the baking soda. We used 10 red drops and 6 yellow drops for orange lava.
5. Add a few drops of dish soap. This step is completely optional but does give the lava more volume.
6. Place vinegar in a container that will comfortably allow kids to pour it into the volcano bottle.
7. Start pouring vinegar into your LEGO® volcano. Try to pour from a few inches above the opening of the bottle to allow for the volcano to really erupt!
8. Alternate adding baking soda and vinegar as long as you want. Your volcano can erupt over and over again.
9. To clean up simply rinse everything off and leave out to dry.

Skills:
Science Experiment

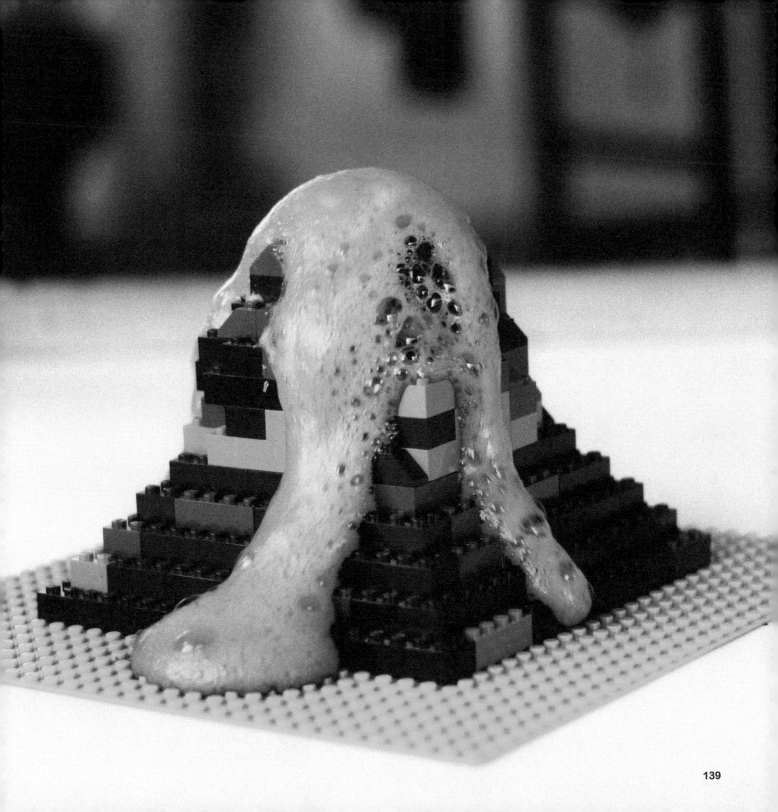

Zipline

Materials / Supplies

- Various bricks and pieces including plates and a minifigure.
- Small clothes line pulley (hardware store)
- Clothesline (hardware store)

Instructions

There are a bunch of great ways to mix up this learning experience. You can alter the height of the rope or you can build different sized or weighted creations. Why not try out different types of ropes like parachute cord or ribbon? What changes? What makes the zipline faster or slower? How about a LEGO® zipline race? Set up two ropes, grab a stopwatch, and see which one is fastest.

Use this LEGO® zipline to learn about friction, gravity, planes and inclines. Learn about physics while having a great time playing and creating. This is an awesome educational activity that gets kids moving, thinking, problem solving, and building. Test your engineering skills to build the best LEGO® zipline.

1. Get creative. You can use our model as a starting point, but you can really create anything you want.
2. Thread the pulley onto the clothesline.
3. Attach the clothesline at two points. One should be higher.
4. Attach a minifigure.
5. Send your creation down the zipline! Repeat over and over.

Skills:
Engineering

Line Art

Materials / Supplies

- Black construction paper
- White chalk
- Variety of 2x2 bricks

Instructions

1. Draw lines and squiggles on the black construction paper.
2. Use 2x2 bricks to follow the line to the end.

Skills:
Fine Motor, Hand-eye Coordination

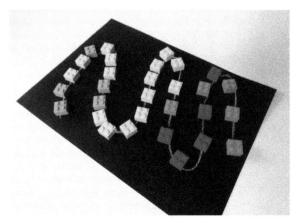

Making Shapes

Materials / Supplies

- 6 purple 8x1 plates (diamond)
- 6 yellow 6x1 plates (square)
- 3 light blue 6x1 plates (triangle)
- 2 black 8x1 plates (rectangle)
- 2 black 4x1 plates
- 8 green 3x1 plates (circle)

Instructions

1. Use the color coded plates to build the shapes as shown in the images.

Extensions for this activity:
1. Use the shapes to make new designs
2. Use the shapes to trace with on a sheet of paper remove them, shuffle, then find the shape that matches to the one on the paper.

Skills:
Shapes, Logic

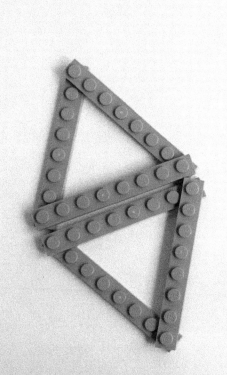

Measuring Weight

Materials / Supplies

- Kitchen scale
- Bricks in 2x2 and 2x4 (any variety will work but just have enough of each handy)
- Measuring cups
- Objects to compare to LEGO® weight. We used a lemon, a ball, and a small bottle of water

Instructions

This activity is an invitation to explore math concepts such as volume, size, and measuring weight. You can talk about the different types of weight measurements such as ounces, grams, kilograms, pounds, or stones.

You can also learn about matter. Everything has matter and takes up space. Small amounts of matter can be very heavy and take up little space, whereas some large amounts of matter can be very light and take up lots of space. Compare 8 ounces of water to the same amount of LEGO®. Which one takes up more space?

Bring out a conversion chart for older kids to use. Younger kids will have a blast testing out the different objects, as well as comparing and contrasting them. Try out as many objects as you can find. How much LEGO® does it take to make a 1 pound? How many pounds of LEGO® do you have? Measure out equal amounts for everyone.

1. Set out the scale and show kids how to turn it on. Determine what measurement of weight you want to use. We chose ounces.
2. Set out bricks, measuring cups, and objects.
3. Encourage kids to explore the various weights of everything on the table. How much does the lemon weigh? How many 2x2 bricks does it take to equal the weight of the lemon? Fill the measuring cups with water. How many bricks does it take to equal a 1/4 cup of water? Compare and contrast the objects. Have fun exploring!

Skills:
Math, Measurements

Mini Robots

Materials / Supplies

- Egg carton lid or tray for sorting parts
- Small parts including any kind of angled plates, connectors, hinges, flat tiles, studs, 1x1s, holders of various kinds, tooth plates, bricks with knobs, nose cones, round bricks 1x1, knob plates, and studs.
- 2x2, 2x3, 2x4 bricks in various colors
- Accessories such as magnifying glasses, antennas, or gear sticks

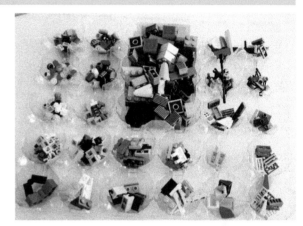

Instructions

Design and build mini robots for a fun STEM learning activity. Robots are full of technology, but they have to start with a good design and a model. Test your design skills by sketching robots. Use your building and engineering skills to make your design into a LEGO® robot. Not quite what you thought? Go back to the drawing board, problem solve, and rebuild your robot.

Create a story for your robot. What can it do? Why is it useful? Where would it be used? When would it be needed? Who would use the robot?

Build another robot but this time work backwards and start with the questions first. Design and build a robot to fit your answers.

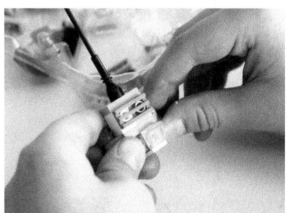

1. Gather your tiniest, smallest LEGO® pieces that often fall to the bottom of the bucket. Building mini robots is the perfect opportunity to learn how to use these small parts to create awesome details. Sort out these items into the lid of an egg carton or a divided tray.
2. Build your mini robot! The goal is to make your mini robot as detailed as possible by adding small parts.
3. Practice using different connectors, angled plates, and bricks with knobs to build intricate details.

Skills:
Engineering

Minifigures Bath

Materials / Supplies

- Minifigures
- Small container
- Soap and water
- Toothbrush or sponges
- Towels

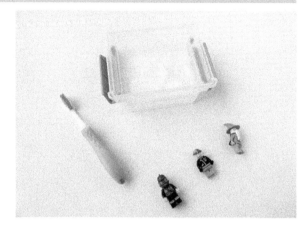

Instructions

Giving minifigures a bath and scrubbing with a toothbrush is an excellent way for kids to work on fine motor and practical life skills, while also getting some clean sensory input.

1. Collect some minifigures that could use cleaning.
2. Fill a small container with warm, soapy water and set out on a table with a toothbrush, sponge and towel.
3. Invite child(ren) to scrub the minifigures using the soapy water and toothbrush or sponge.
4. Set wet minifigures on a towel to dry.

Skills:
Fine Motor

More, Less or Equal

Materials / Supplies

- 2 baseplates
- 12 minifigures
- Dice

Instructions

Playing More, Less or Equal with minifigures is a simple way for kids to practice counting, subitising and comparing quantities.

1. Set up two baseplates and a dozen minifigures with a number die.
2. Invite your child(ren) to play More, Less or Equal.
3. To play More, Less or Equal, children take turns rolling the number die and counting out that many minifigures, standing on the baseplate.
4. Children then compare the amount of minifigures on the two baseplates and answer the question if their baseplate has more minifigures, less minifigures or an equal amount of minifigures.

Skills:
Math

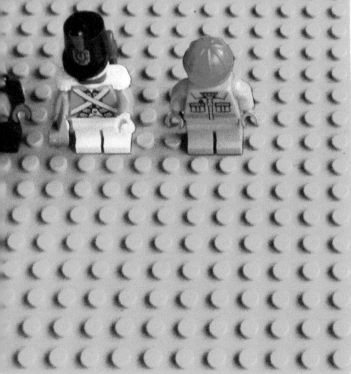

100 Board

Materials / Supplies

- 100 tan tiles
- Green 32x32 stud baseplate
- Flat blue bricks
- Fine point permanent marker
- Ice cube tray (for tile storage)
- Dry erase marker (to erase permanent marker)

Instructions

Using a 100 board made with LEGO® is a fun and hands-on way for kids to learn math skills. It can be used to practice counting, number recognition, identifying number patterns and many other math skills.

1. Using a fine point permanent marker, write the numbers 1-100 on each of the tan tiles.
2. Sort the tiles into an ice cube tray for easy storage.
3. Create a 20x20 stud square on the green baseplate using the blue flat bricks.
4. Children can then fill in the square by placing the numbered tiles in numerical order.

Skills:
Math

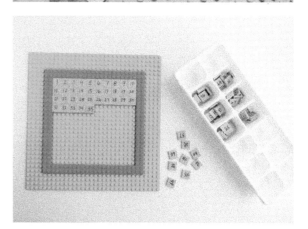

1	2	3	4	5	6	7	8	9	10
11	12	13	14	15	16	17	18	19	20
21	22	23	24	25	26	27	28	29	30
31	32	33	34	35	36	37	38	39	40
41	42	43	44	45	46	47	48	49	50
51	52	53	54	55	56	57	58	59	60
61	62	63	64	65	66	67	68	69	70
71	72	73	74	75	76	77	78	79	80
81	82	83	84	85	86	87	88	89	90
91	92	93	94	95	96	97	98	99	100

My Emotions

Materials / Supplies

- Various bricks to complete a man
- Dry erase marker
- Cloth wipe off marker

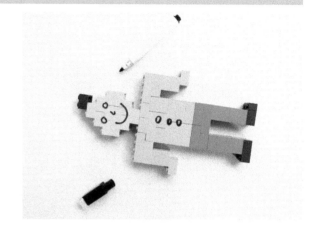

Instructions

1. This is a free build activity. Have your child build a person. Use the images as inspiration.
2. Draw on the man to express emotions that the child is currently feeling or would like to discuss.
3. This figure is also great for roleplaying.

Skills:
Emotions, Imagination

Nesting Boxes

Materials / Supplies

- Random bricks
- Random plates

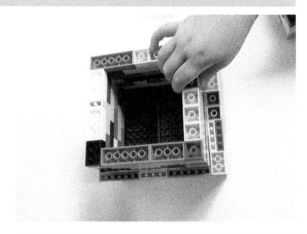

Instructions

1. Build a small square out of bricks 4 rows high.
2. Around the first square, build another square 5 rows high.
3. Again another square 6 rows high.
4. One last square around the square again, 7 rows high.
5. Use your plates to close the top of the squares.
6. Stack your squares bigger on the bottom to smaller on the top then invert to nest them into each other.
7. Use the 3 bigger squares to do a large, medium and small brick sort activity

Skills:
Engineering, Logic, Sorting

Number Bonds

Materials / Supplies

- Large baseplate
- Long bricks that are 1 stud wide
- 10 or more 1X1 bricks for counters

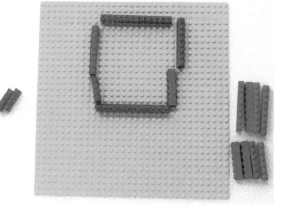

Instructions

1. Build a large square near the top center of the base plate, 13 studs by 14 studs.
2. Construct two smaller squares starting 5 studs below the large square, 8 studs by 8.
3. Add a brick to link the two small squares to the large one.
4. To use your number bond board, take turns adding 1X1 counter bricks to the two small rectangles then use bricks to make the total number of counters in the large rectangle. Due to the shape of LEGO® bricks it is best to make your numbers in the style of a digital watch, with all right angles. You can add in a game die or number cards to help determine which numbers to do each time.

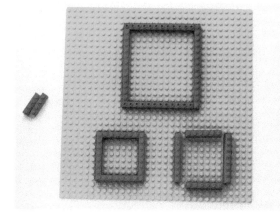

Skills:
Math

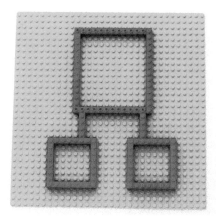

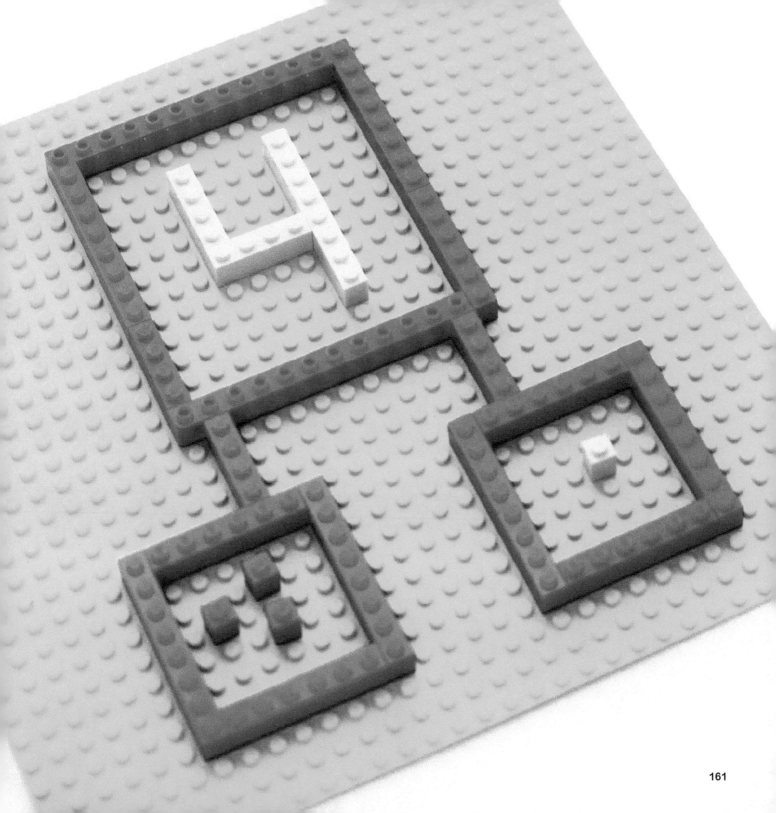

Number Line Counting Game

Materials / Supplies

- 2x8 or 2x4 bricks
- 2x2 bricks
- 2 baseplates
- Minifigures
- Dice

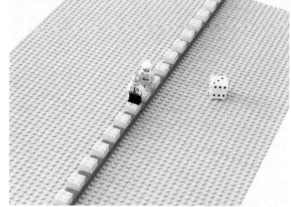

Instructions

While playing this hands-on math game, children will practice counting and one to one correspondence. They will also learn various social skills such as taking turns and being nice whether you win or lose.

Instructions:
1. Put the 2x8 or 2x4 bricks end to end across two baseplates so that they form a long line.
2. Place the 2x2 bricks at equal increments along the line. Each one represents a number on the number line. You can use a dry-erase marker or chalk marker to write the number on the side of the brick.
3. Place the minifigures on the table right before the first brick on the line. Each player will need one to serve as their game piece.
4. Players will take turns rolling the game die and moving that many spaces on the number line with their minifigure.
5. The first player to reach the end of the number line wins!

Skills:
Math

Patterning Printable

Materials / Supplies

- Patterning printable
- 16 Green 2x2
- 18 Blue 2x2
- 17 Red 2x2
- 21 Yellow 2x2

Printable
See Page
208

Instructions

1. Print out the printable on cardstock. You can either leave it as a sheet or cut it into strips.
2. Place a color brick on each square and complete the sequence.

Skills:
Logic, Puzzle, Fine Motor

Minifigure Search & Build

Materials / Supplies

- 3 balls of playdough
- 3 minifigures
- Minifigures accessories

Instructions

Digging through playdough searching for LEGO® minifigure pieces to build is a fun, sensory way for kids to work on fine motor skills. Kids can also use their imagination to creatively build silly minifigures or work to match up all the correct pieces for each minifigure.

1. Roll 3 balls of play dough and flatten it out.
2. Add some minifigure pieces and roll the playdough into a ball.
3. Invite children to dig into each ball of playdough and search for the minifigure pieces.
4. Then children can put together the minifigures with the found pieces.

Skills:
Fine Motor

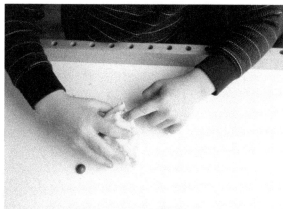

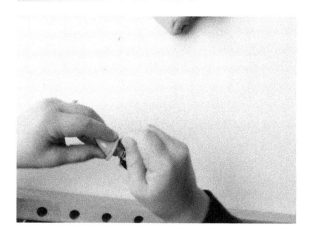

Puzzle Mat

Materials / Supplies

- Bricks of various sizes
- Paper
- Pencil
- Painter's tape

Instructions

1. Make a design with bricks of various sizes. Do this with the bricks upside-down. Designs can be as small or large as you want, depending on the age and abilities of the children participating.
2. As shown in the picture, use painter's tape or another removable tape to hold the pieces together.
3. Flip the taped design over and trace the outline on a piece of paper with a pencil.
4. Repeat steps 1-3 several times until you have a piece of paper with several different shapes traced onto it.
5. Remove all the tape from the backs of the bricks and place them all in a pile.
6. Invite your child to fill in the shapes on the paper with bricks from the pile.

Skills:
Critical Thinking, Problem Solving, Hand-eye Coordination, Fine Motor.

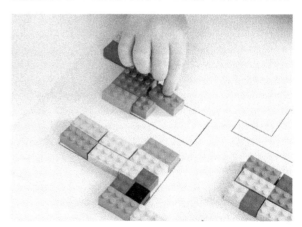

Rainbow Mobile

Materials / Supplies

- One 2X4 brick for every color of the rainbow
- One 4X12 flat base piece
- 2 sets of wide wheels
- 2 white 2X2 bricks
- 2 white window bricks
- 1 steering wheel
- 1 minifigure

Instructions

1. Snap the wheels onto the flat base piece.
2. Attach the color bricks in rainbow order (red, orange, yellow, green, blue, indigo, violet.) Building note: the first and last bricks hang half way off, as pictured.
3. Attach the 2 white 2X2 bricks on the red side to symbolize the front, or beginning. Add the two window pieces on top of them, then add the steering wheel. Your Rainbow Mobile is ready for its driver.
4. For children who are just learning colors, you can take turns pointing and naming the colors in order. For children who have already learned the colors in order, you can challenge your child to add the colors to the base in the correct order. This activity is perfect for those without enough bricks to construct a full rainbow but still want to practice colors and ROYGBIV order.

Skills:
Colors

Removable LEGO® Wall

Materials / Supplies

- Duplo baseplate or LEGO® extra large baseplate
- Bungee cords (we used mini 10 inch ones), see alternatives below
- Drill
- Easel

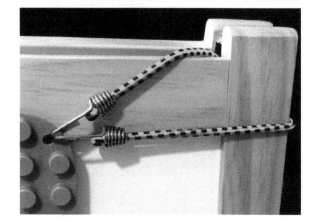

Alternatives:
If you don't want to use bungee cords you can try a couple other options. They still assume you will drill holes in the plates:

1. You can tie the base plates onto your easel with heavy twine.
2. You can also attach 3M Wire Command Hooks to your easel, depending on the surface of your easel, or to your walls. These have special double sided adhesive that can be removed without damaging most surfaces. The best way to do that would be to attach the command strip to your wall, press on the wire hook and hang the base plate on the hooks using the drilled holes.
3. If you are not concerned about removing them you can attach them directly to your walls more permanently with screws.

Instructions

1. Using a drill bit that is slightly larger than the thickness of the bungee cord hook, drill holes in 2-4 corners of your base plate, depending on if you plan to attach it on two corners or all four.
2. Using the bungee cords, hook one side in one hole and wrap it over the top, around the side, and back to the same hole to attach it. Repeat with the other top corner and then attach the bottom two corners similarly around the bottom edge of the easel board, if desired.
3. Play! Taking a toy to a vertical plane helps kids develop core and shoulder muscles, as well as develop correct wrist position for when it is time to start writing. Allow your kids to play freely or use this to practice things like color sorting or counting.

Skills:
Fine Motor Skills

Retelling Simple Stories

Materials / Supplies

- A Variety of LEGO® (depends on the story you are retelling)

Instructions

1. This is the perfect activity to do after you read your favorite story with your kids. It is perfect for sequencing, reading comprehension, and even language development.
2. Start with a simple story such as 3 Little Pigs and encourage your children to make the beginning, middle, and end of the story using the bricks they have.
3. In addition to making the setting (the houses) encourage your child to create the characters for the story they are retelling.
4. Once your scenes are built, your child can retell the story using the props and characters. You can ask comprehension questions and they can use the pieces to act out the answers.
5. There are so many simple nursery rhymes and fables, pick one you and your child are familiar with before trying something more elaborate or difficult.

Skills:
Reading Comprehension, Art, Retelling, Language Development

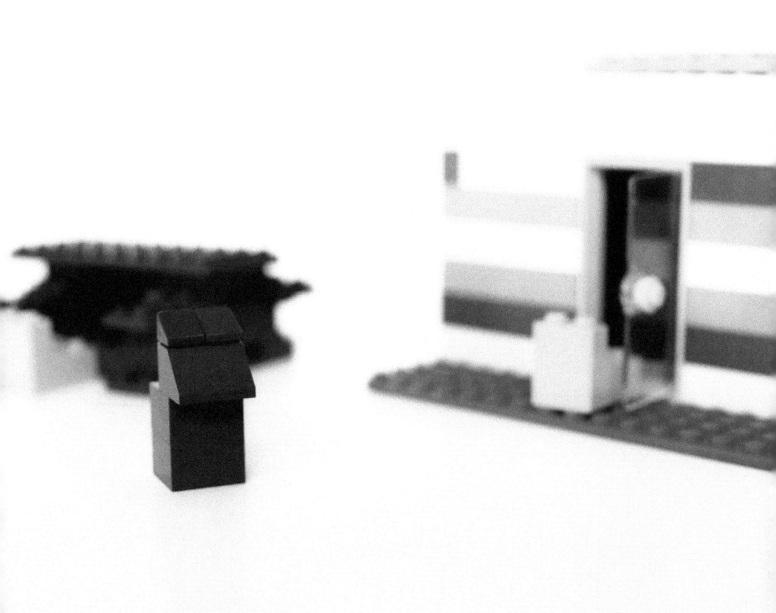

Shaving Cream Search & Build

Materials / Supplies

- Shallow bin
- Shaving cream
- Small container of water
- Towels
- Various bricks and small parts

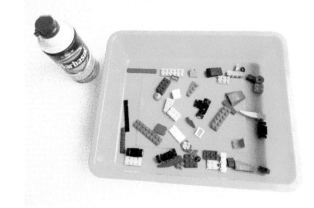

Instructions

This is an open-ended sensory LEGO® activity, so kids can use their imagination to build whatever they want! It is also a great fine motor exercise.

1. Place various bricks and small parts in the bottom of a shallow bin.
2. Cover the LEGO® with a layer of shaving cream.
3. Set out the shaving cream bin, a container of water, and towels on a table.
4. Invite the child(ren) to dig into the shaving cream bin and search for the LEGO®.
5. Once the bricks and parts have been found they can be rinsed off in the container of water and dried with a towel.
6. Then the child(ren) can build with the bricks and parts they found.

Skills:
Sensory, Fine Motor

Sight Word Towers

Materials / Supplies

- 2x2 Duplo bricks
- 1x8 Duplo plate
- Chalk marker or dry erase marker

Instructions

Building these sight word towers is a fun, hands-on way to commit sight words to memory.

1. Pick two or three words you want to work on.
2. Write each letter of each word on a brick with a chalk marker and repeat this 5-8 times. So if you are practicing the word "the" you will write "t" on 5-8 bricks, "h" on 5-8 bricks and "e" on 5-8 bricks. Do this for each word.
3. Put all of the bricks in a pile.
4. Put the bricks needed to spell one sight word on the 1x8 plate. Do this for each word you are working on.
5. Invite your child to repeat the words over and over again with the bricks in the pile.

Skills:
Reading

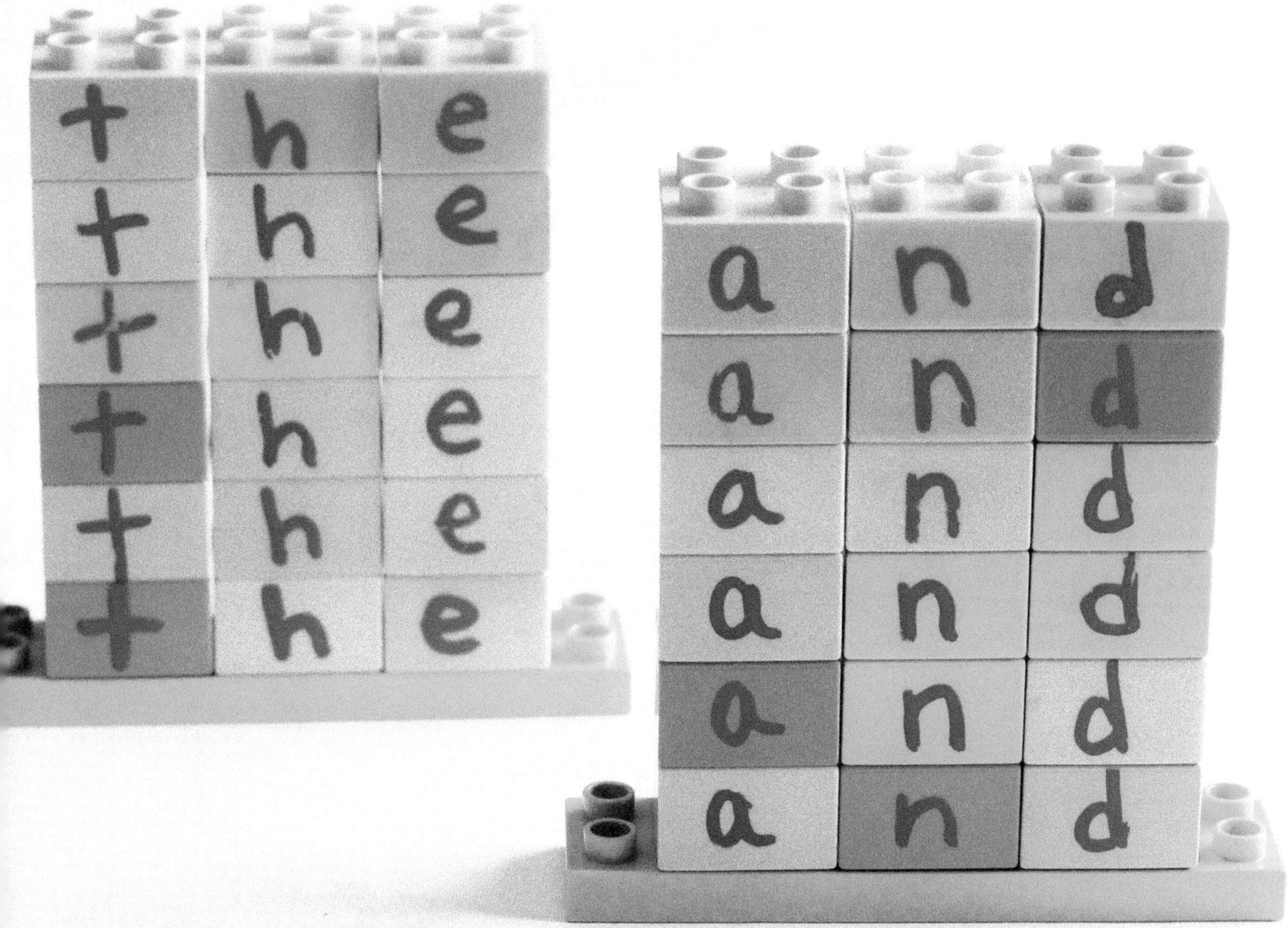
the
the
the
the
the
the
and
and
and
and
and
and

Simple Addition to 20

Materials / Supplies

- 20 minifigures
- Addition to 20 playmat

Printable
See Page
208

Instructions

1. Using the minifigures, place the desired number of figures on the table.
2. Divide the total into two sets (5+6) and then color in the corresponding minifigures to represent the numbers used to make the combination.
3. Do this for each number up to 20.
4. This activity can be done multiple times with different answers since there are many ways to make up each of these numbers. The goal is to let children see the relationship between groups of ten and the numbers they are building.

Skills:
Counting, Simple Addition, Number Writing to 20, Fine Motor

Making Numbers with Le[

6 + 5	=	**11**	
4 + 8	=	**12**	
+	=	**13**	
+	=	**14**	
+	=	**15**	
+	=	**16**	
+	=	**17**	
+	=	**18**	
+	=	**19**	
+	=	**20**	

Simple Fractions

Materials / Supplies

- 2 colors of bricks.
- We recommend the following bricks:
- 2 2x8 bricks (This represents the whole in each color)
- 8 1x2 bricks (4 of each color)
- 24 2x2 bricks (12 of each color)
- *You can use other combinations as you see in the pictures, this is a great starting point for beginners.

Instructions

1. This activity is perfect for early elementary and children just starting to learn about fractions.
2. Discuss with your child how the 2x8 represents the "Whole" or "One" and each row of pegs (1x2) represents an eighth of the whole.
3. Slowly build a new row, changing only one 1x2 brick at a time. So the second row will be 1/8 of the new color and 7/8 of the original color.
4. This activity is great for representing whole numbers as fractions. You can do this with a 2x6, 2x10, 1x5, and so on. The idea is to show the individual pieces that make the whole.

Skills:
Fractions, Patterning, Spatial Reasoning, Fine Motor

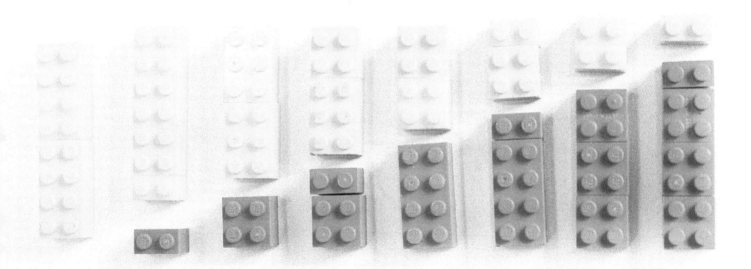

Sinking Materials in Water

Materials / Supplies

- Bricks in various sizes
- Various materials to place the bricks on in the water - example include: aluminum foil, wax paper, plastic wrap, plates, bowls, silicone baking liners, etc.
- Large container of water

Instructions

While exploring, children will begin to learn about sinking and floating. They will develop critical thinking and problem solving skills. They will compare amounts and begin to understand the concept of greater than or less than. They will explore various materials and begin to see how those items compare to each other. They will even be given the opportunity to test ideas and analyze outcomes at their own level of ability.

1. Place a piece of aluminum foil in the water.
2. One by one, add bricks to the top of it.
3. Keep adding bricks until the piece of aluminum foil begins to sink under the water.
4. Repeat this with all the materials you are testing.
5. Ask questions that will encourage your child to think critically about what is happening. Here are some ideas!

Questions to Ask Before the Experiment:
   *Which material do you think will hold the most bricks before sinking? Why?
   *Which material do you think will hold the least amount of bricks? Why?

Questions to Ask During the Experiment:
*Why do you think that happened?
*Is there any way we could change this so it would hold more bricks?

Questions to Ask After the Experiment:
   *Why do you think _____ held more bricks than the other items we tested?
   *Why do you think _____ held less than other items we tested?
   *Do you think it would matter if we tried bricks that were all the same size instead of different sizes?
    * What if we changed the size of the materials we tested?

Encourage your child to test their theories. Test an item or two again with the same sized bricks. Did your result change? Try bigger or smaller materials. How did that result differ from last time?

I set this up as an investigation for my preschooler, so I wasn't concerned with explaining all of the science behind everything. I simply invited him to explore and investigate what was happening.

Skills:
Critical Thinking, Problem Solving

Size Matching

Materials / Supplies

- 1 baseplate
- Assortment of bricks

Instructions

1. Make 3 long rectangle shapes down one side of the baseplate.
2. Start the copy next to them so that it can be completed.
3. Complete the shapes to match using various sized bricks.

Skills:
Logic, Puzzles, Fine Motor

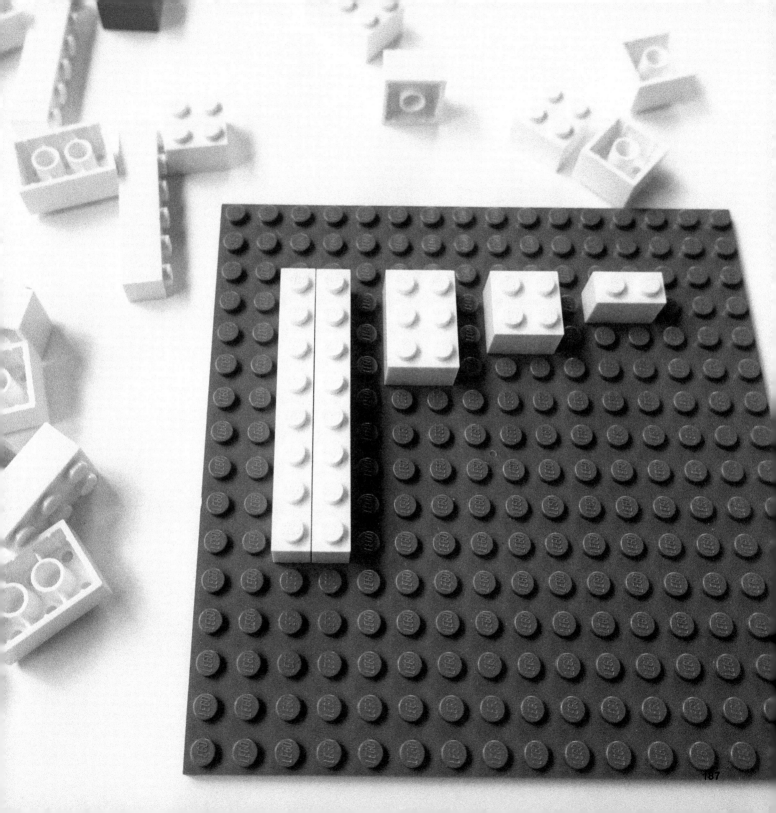

Skip Counting

Materials / Supplies

- 5-10 small clear plastic cups
- Dry erase marker
- 20-100 1x1 bricks depending on numbers you are counting

Instructions

1. Draw numbers on the cups.
2. Make towers of the same numbers you wrote on the cups.
3. Add the correct number of towers per cup to equal that number.

Skills:
Math

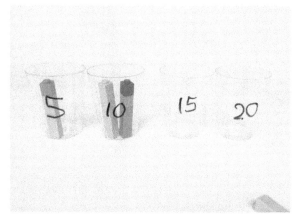

Spanish Numbers Match Up

Materials / Supplies

- 1-4 sets of 10 same sized, same color, bricks
- Fine-tip permanent marker
- Baseplate (optional for the number line variation)
- Rubbing alcohol for cleanup

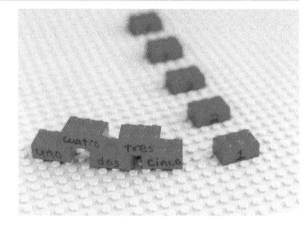

Instructions

1. Using your permanent marker write the words or numbers that you want to study, one word on the face of each brick. Spanish numbers are used here but you may adapt it for any language or vocabulary. You can use digits, Spanish numbers, English numbers or numbered dots and work with 1-5 or as high as you like.

2. Once they are all written out, show your child how to match the bricks, for example 1 with uno.

3. Variations:

Number Line: Place the digit bricks in a number line on a baseplate. Ask your child to match up the matching Spanish words in order.

Number Tower Matchup: If you have prepared bricks with English, Spanish, digits and dots you can ask your child to make towers of all four matching bricks for each number.

Counting Tower: Using only the Spanish bricks, have your child stack them in numerical order. Spanish Math: Add bricks with number signs to the mix and you can do basic math in Spanish.

Skills:
Foreign Language, Math

Sun Clock

Materials / Supplies

- 1 baseplate in a light color
- 15 1x1 bricks
- 11 1x1 studs

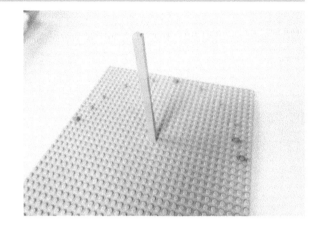

Instructions

1. Make a longer tower of your 1x1 bricks and attach to the center of the baseplate.
2. Find a spot that gets sun the entire day and put your sun clock down.
3. Use the 1x1 studs to make where the shadow is every hour of the day.
4. Pair this activity with telling time or learning about the sun ideas.

Skills:
Observation

Surprise LEGO® Bath Bombs

Materials / Supplies

Dry ingredients:
* Baking soda – 1 cup
* Citric acid – 1/2 cup
* Corn starch – 1/2 cup
* Epsom salt – 1/2 cup

Wet Ingredients:
* Water: just a spritz (enough to just dampen the dough)
* Essential oils
* 2 tablespoons almond oil
* Food coloring (optional)

LEGO® of Choice:
* Disassembled Mini Set or Minifigure
* Ice molds or cupcake molds

Instructions

1. Start by mixing together all of your dry ingredients into one bowl. It's a good idea to get everything mixed as evenly as you can.
2. Add in your wet ingredients and stir gently. You will see a slight reaction but not a lot.
3. Then using your spray bottle, spritz your dough with just a little bit of water. (You don't want too much or your mixture will start to react.) You want the dough to be moldable but not mushy.
4. Fill your mold with the mixture half way, put the minifigure in the middle and fill the other side with more mixture. Make sure to firmly press the mold and then set the ball to dry.
5. Let your bath bombs dry overnight before using letting your kids bathe with their bath bombs to release their minifigure.

Skills:
Science, Measurement, Sensory Integration (Tactile and Proprioceptive)

Telling Time Clock

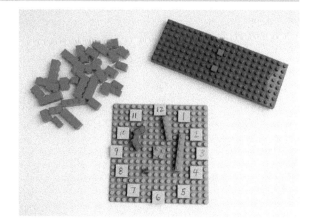

Materials / Supplies

- Small square baseplate
- 12 2x2 tiles
- Permanent fine point marker
- 1x4 plate
- 1x6 plate
- 1x4 hinge plate
- Turntable plate
- 1x1 round plate
- Red bricks in various sizes
- Red 1x1 plates
- Gray plates for digital clock

Instructions

Using the Telling Time LEGO® Clock is a fun, hands-on way for kids to learn to read an analog clock.

1. Write the numbers 1-12 on each of the 2x2 tiles.
2. Then using the plates and tiles listed, build an analog clock face with spinning hour and minute hands.
3. With the additional plates, build a digital clock face. Make sure to have enough space for four numbers.
4. To use the Telling Time LEGO® Clock, have the child(ren) spin the hands on the analog clock face, and build the numbers onto the digital clock face.

Skills:
Telling Time

Tetris

Materials / Supplies

- 1 light color baseplate
- 18 green 2x1 bricks (z)
- 18 light blue 2x1 bricks (other z)
- 18 dark blue 2x1 bricks (L)
- 18 yellow 2x1 bricks (other L)
- 18 purple 2x1 bricks (I)
- 6 red 2x2 bricks (square)
- 6 red 2x1 bricks
- 6 orange 3x1 bricks (short T)
- 6 1x1 orange bricks
- 6 2x2 orange bricks
- Assortment of 1x white bricks for the boarders

Instructions

1. On the baseplate make a container area with 10 studs for the tetris game plus 2 extra containers on the sides to contain the game pieces. Define these areas by using the assortment of 1x white bricks.
2. Construct your game pieces to resemble those in the images. You will make 6 of each type of game piece.
3. Play the game by randomly selecting a game piece to place in the grid.
4. Play this game with a friend and hand each other peices and take turns to complete the tetris puzzle.

Skills:
Logic, Construction, Hand-eye Coordination

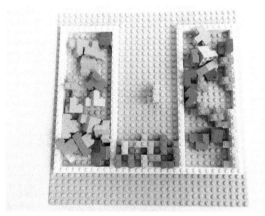

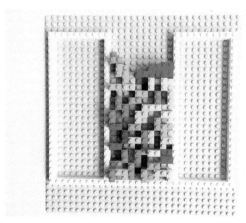

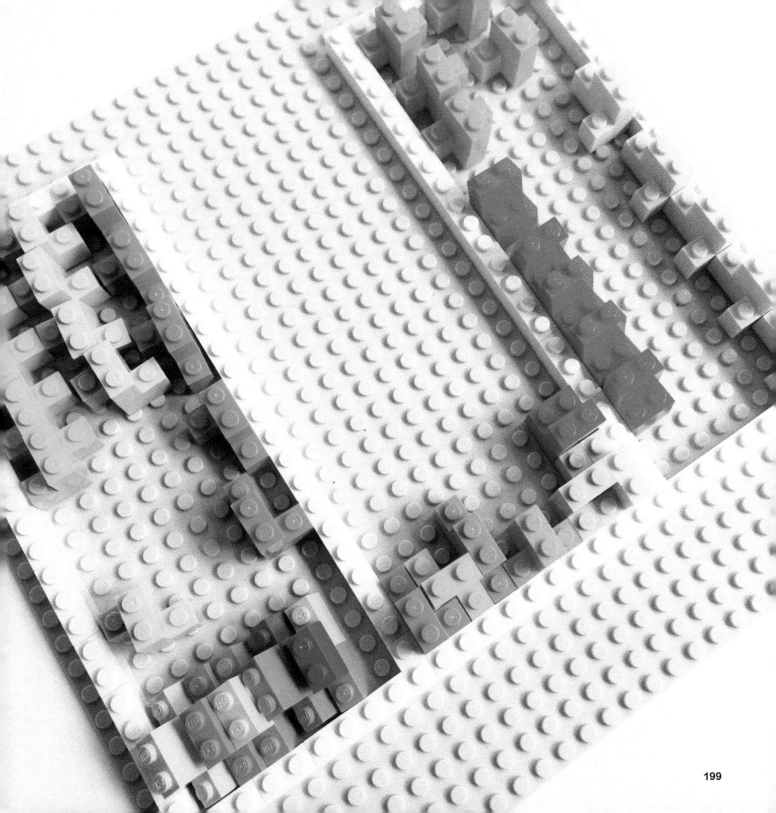

Tower Counting Game

Materials / Supplies

- Duplo bricks of varying sizes
- Dice

Instructions

When children use the game die they learn to identify numbers by sight without counting. They will also practice counting as they place the bricks on the tower. When building their tower they will need to use critical thinking skills and strategizing skills to decide how to balance the tower while still making it high enough to win the game.

1. Set a certain amount of turns each person will take. A good starting point is 10 turns per person.
2. Players will take turns rolling the game die and putting that many bricks on their tower.
3. The person with the highest tower after all turns have been taken is the winner.
4. If a tower falls before all turns have been taken, that player is out.

Skills:
Counting, Critical Thinking

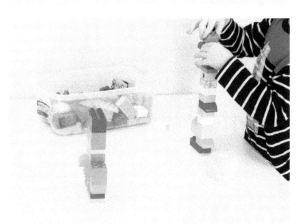

Tracing Letters

Materials / Supplies

- 2x2 bricks
- Paper
- Marker

Instructions

Children will become aware of letters and their structure. They will begin to identify letters by name. It is also a great way to introduce letter sounds and beginning sound identification.

1. Draw or type/print one letter on each sheet of paper.
2. Your child will use the bricks to trace around the letter.
3. If you want, you can also encourage them to trace it in the same way you would write it.
4. Talk about the name of the letter and the sound it makes. You can even talk about words that start with that letter.

Skills:
Letter Recognition

Under the Sea

Materials / Supplies

- Blue baseplate
- Green and brown 1x1 bricks
- Green and brown 1x1 studs
- Random items such as skeleton parts, gems, eyes, gears
- Fin like bricks

Instructions

1. Create a scene of under the ocean by making seaweeds and caves.
2. Create fish like creatures for your scene.
3. Inspire the imagination by making up a story about what the diver might find under the sea (crabs, fish, sea shells, starfish and even treasure).
4. This idea is great paired with other under the sea studies or arts.

Skills:
Imagination, Storytelling

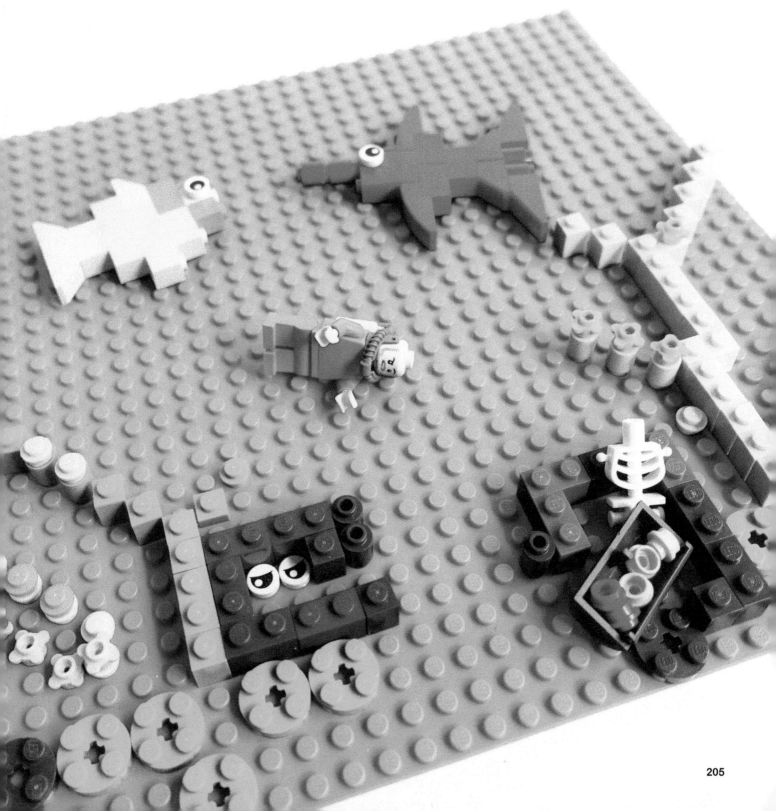

Wind Powered Car

Materials / Supplies

- Wheels and wheel parts
- Small plates
- Bricks that will work for holding a sail
- Notecards for sails
- Tray of small decorative parts
- Tape
- Fan or other wind source

Instructions

Building a wind powered car with LEGO® is a great way for kids to practice science, technology, engineering and math (S.T.E.M.) skills.

1. Set out the supplies and invite children to design and build a wind powered car using only the parts provided.
2. Test out the wind cars using a fan or other wind source.
3. Make adjustments to wind car designs and try again.
4. As a final test, have a wind car race!

Skills:
S.T.E.M.

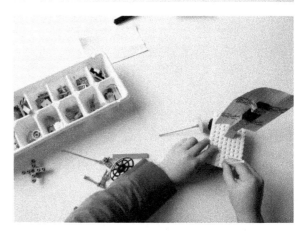

Printables

Pages with printables:

Download all printables here:

https://goo.gl/GKmvm6

Page 18

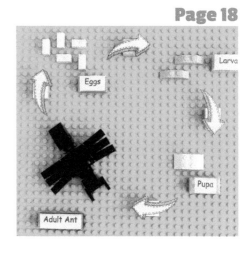

Page 26

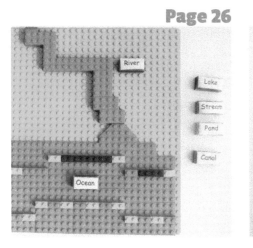

Page 36

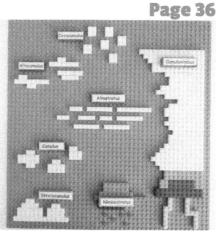

Page 66

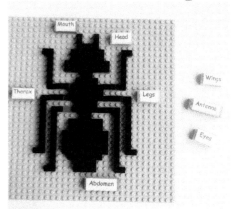

Page 70

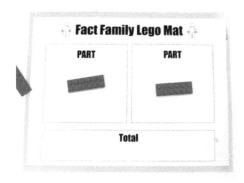

Page 90

Page 92

Page 106

Page 164

Page 180

CPSIA information can be obtained
at www.ICGtesting.com
Printed in the USA
BVHW062342160519
548424BV00011B/68/P